LEARNING ALLOWED

EMERALD STUDIES IN CHILD CENTRED PRACTICE

Series Editor: Sam Frankel, King's University College, Western University, Canada

Emerald Studies in Child Centred Practice: Voice, Collaboration and Change seeks to reposition the place of childhood studies as a discipline, highlighting its social value. This series explores the application of theories from childhood studies in practice. It highlights the place, purpose and power of these theories to inform practice and seek to shape a child-centred approach across the settings within which children live and experience their everyday lives – schools, families, the law and the care system. Uniquely, books in the series will not only draw on academic insight but also include the perspectives of both practitioners and children. The series makes the case for the need for a shared dialogue as a foundation for re-imagining practice.

This new series offers a new and valuable dimension to childhood studies with relevance for how wider society comes to engage with it. Indeed, it offers a chance for childhood studies to increase its presence in society – to demonstrate how an awareness of children's agency and the constructed nature of society can positively influence discourse and debate – with the hope that this can increasingly shape policy and practice and add value to children's everyday experiences.

Proposals are welcome for the series that align to this goal and help us to develop and grow childhood studies. This series is particularly keen to explore multifaceted aspects of children's lives, such as schooling, home lives, children's rights, child protection, activism, and more.

LEARNING ALLOWED: CHILDREN, COMMUNITIES AND LIFELONG LEARNING IN A CHANGING WORLD

BY

SAM FRANKEL
King's University College, Western University, Canada

AND

CAROLINE E. WHALLEY
The Elliot Foundation Academy Trust, UK

United Kingdom – North America – Japan – India
Malaysia – China

Emerald Publishing Limited
Emerald Publishing, Floor 5, Northspring, 21-23 Wellington Street, Leeds LS1 4DL

First edition 2024

Copyright © 2024 Sam Frankel and Caroline E. Whalley.
Published under exclusive licence by Emerald Publishing Limited.

Reprints and permissions service
Contact: www.copyright.com

No part of this book may be reproduced, stored in a retrieval system, transmitted in any form or by any means electronic, mechanical, photocopying, recording or otherwise without either the prior written permission of the publisher or a licence permitting restricted copying issued in the UK by The Copyright Licensing Agency and in the USA by The Copyright Clearance Center. Any opinions expressed in the chapters are those of the authors. Whilst Emerald makes every effort to ensure the quality and accuracy of its content, Emerald makes no representation implied or otherwise, as to the chapters' suitability and application and disclaims any warranties, express or implied, to their use.

British Library Cataloguing in Publication Data
A catalogue record for this book is available from the British Library

ISBN: 978-1-80117-401-5 (Print)
ISBN: 978-1-80117-400-8 (Online)
ISBN: 978-1-80117-402-2 (Epub)

Printed and bound by CPI Group (UK) Ltd, Croydon, CR0 4YY

INVESTOR IN PEOPLE

SF: Moira, Ruari, Rosie, Maria and Elsie
CW: Adam and Alex
and all those we have learned with.

TABLE OF CONTENTS

List of Figures	ix
Foreword	xi
Acknowledgements	xiii

1. We Need to Talk About… Allowing Learning! — 1
2. An Approach – To Allowing Learning — 9

The Connected Learner in Theory

3. Who Is a Learner? — 33
4. What Is Learning For? — 53
5. How We Can Allow Learning: Impact of Self and 'Other' on Our Learning Identities — 69

The Connected Learner in Practice

Introducing the Connected Learner in Practice

6. 'P' – Power Up Your Thinking — 93
7. 'L' – Nurture a 'Learn to Be' Culture — 103
8. 'U' – Unify Your Language — 113
9. 'G' – Grow Meaningful Opportunities — 125
10. 'IN' – Inspire Lead Learners — 133
11. The Individual as a Connected Learner — 141
12. Enduring Connections – Learning Allowed — 159

References — 163
Index — 177

LIST OF FIGURES

Chapter 1
Figure 1.   Solving Tame Problems.   5

Chapter 2
Figure 2.   Responding to Our Changing World.   10
Figure 3.   Global Influences and Impacts.   11
Figure 4.   The Seven Ages of Learning.   13
Figure 5.   Connectivity Continuum.   14
Figure 6.   Pressures for Learners.   27
Figure 7.   Connection Continuum.   29
Figure 8.   Influences on Our Sense of Connectivity.   30

Chapter 3
Figure 9.   Chapter 3 Overview.   34
Figure 10.   One-Way and Two-Way Arrows.   47
Figure 11.   Identifying Forces on Our Personal Lives.   49

Chapter 4
Figure 12.   Chapter 4 Overview.   54
Figure 13.   Learning Across Time and Space.   60

Chapter 5
Figure 14.   Chapter 5 Overview.   70
Figure 15.   Rule-Based Learning.   71
Figure 16.   Happiness and Learning.   77
Figure 17.   Balancing Our Sense of Power.   80
Figure 18.   Perspectives of Power.   80

Chapter 6
Figure 19.   Impact of Assumptions.   96
Figure 20.   Drawing of Mr Fowler.   97
Figure 21.   Assumption Tracker 1.   98

Figure 22.	Assumption Tracker 2.	99
Figure 23.	Assumption Tracker 3.	99
Figure 24.	Assumption Tracker 4.	100
Figure 25.	Assumption Tracker 5.	100
Figure 26.	Assumption Tracker 6.	101
Figure 27.	Assumption Tracker 7.	101

Chapter 7

| Figure 28. | Taught to Become vs Learn to Be. | 104 |
| Figure 29. | Rhetoric vs Reality Activity. | 109 |

Chapter 8

Figure 30.	Ethos and Value in Practice.	115
Figure 31.	Language for Learning in Practice.	115
Figure 32.	Language for Learning in Pictures.	116
Figure 33.	An Emotional Language for Learning.	120

Chapter 9

| Figure 34. | What is a Learning Opportunity. | 130 |

Chapter 10

| Figure 35. | The Ripple Effect. | 139 |
| Figure 36. | Leadership Attributes. | 140 |

Chapter 11

Figure 37.	Chapter Overview.	142
Figure 38.	Chapter 3 Overview.	143
Figure 39.	Capacity and Potentiality.	144
Figure 40.	Exploring Your Skills.	146
Figure 41.	Chapter 4 Overview.	148
Figure 42.	Chapter 5 Overview.	153
Figure 43.	How Do I Feel Emoji.	154
Figure 44.	Exploring Your Feelings.	154
Figure 45.	Exploring Solutions.	157

Chapter 12

| Figure 46. | The Learning World We Would Like to See. | 160 |

FOREWORD

The internet was going to be a second enlightenment. I remember the hope and anticipatory zeal that burned in the eyes of its prophets. It would democratise learning in unimaginable ways and provide emancipating opportunities for all. Everyone on the planet would have immediate free access to the best recorded thinking of all the 117 billion humans[1] who have lived. How could standing on the shoulders of all the intellectual giants of the past be a bad thing?

Well, we massively underestimated the degree to which videos of kittens would be more interesting than string theory. And whilst the best thinking of the greatest thinkers is mostly available and mostly free, it is buried under a mountain of bullshit and deliberate untruth that is growing exponentially. In the past, every village had an idiot but the worst they could do was to corner you in the pub and bore you for 20 minutes about how the moon landings were faked. With the advent of the internet and its unforeseen facility to promulgate untruth and undermine reasoned debate, they can now become world leaders.

In this light, or rather in this gloom, the challenge to those who would create learners is stark. If we want the world to be better for our children... Dammit, if we want the world to *exist* for our grandchildren, we need to make more people better learners for longer! This challenge transcends formal education systems and threatens nations.

Dr Sam Frankel and Dr Caroline Whalley suggest in this book that great teachers imbue their students with a sense of agency over their own learning processes that they will carry forward for the rest of their lives. But learners can also do it for themselves by understanding their underlying meta-cognitive operations. 'Whether I shall turn out to be the hero of my own life or whether that station will be held by anybody else...'[2], should not be a question in the mind of one who allows themselves to learn and to be a learner.

If we are to save the enlightenment, we need to build on its platform. 'Cogito ergo sum' postulated Descartes. Sartre later challenged, arguing that,

---

1 Source Population Reference Bureau Nov 2022.

2 Opening line of 'David Copperfield', *Charles Dickens*.

'Existence precedes essence'. Sam and Caroline are effectively suggesting that, 'To be is to learn'.

Hugh Greenway
Chief Executive – The Elliot Foundation

ACKNOWLEDGEMENTS

This book really does represent a *Journey* and the interactions that we have had with so many others. Our thanks therefore must start with all those that we have had the chance to learn alongside, whether that be family or friends, children or university students, professionals, parents or researchers. It is these experiences and the conversations, observations, research and training opportunities they created, that we have drawn on in shaping our thinking for 'learning allowed'.

SF: Thanks to those who read early versions of this book and for the ideas they shared – colleagues, students and former students at King's University College, Western University and those connected through EquippingKids. A special thanks to John Fowler who has been so significant in my journey to explore and understand learner experiences over the years.

To Caroline – a very special thank you. Caroline brought her wisdom and clarity of thought to this project, acting as the critical friend I needed to express the ideas that were flying around in my head. The result was a 'learning journey' – where we sought to create knowledge by making sense of our experiences!

CW: Thank you to my dearest friend and alter ego Hugh Greenway, my friends and family plus the gang past and present at The Elliot Foundation who all believe dreams really can come true.

Thank you to Katy and all the team at Emerald for their patience and willingness to work with us.

1

WE NEED TO TALK... ALLOWING LEARNING!

There is an urgent need for a rigorous conversation about the value we attach to 'learning' and 'being a learner'. A mastery of (a) the processes and dimensions of learning and (b) how we make sense of our identity as a learner will advance not only our own capabilities and chances of self-actualisation and happiness, but also the possibilities for wider social transformation.

In this book, we recognise the challenges we face on a local and global level and search for ways to navigate these challenges as we invite you to be part of framing the solution(s) and to embrace the possibilities that this change has to offer. Our message is simple – the way we think about the 'learner' and 'learning' matters. Our sense of identity as learners shapes our motivation and ambitions, our goals and targets, impacting on our private, public and professional lives.

Learning usually centres on children and school. We want to provoke a broader discussion drawing on thinking and research that is child-based and relate this to all stages of our lives. Because of this universal approach, 'teacher', 'facilitator', 'educator' and 'instructor' are used interchangeably referring to any individual who enables 'others' on their learning journey.

Being 'connected' to our learning and possessing a positive identity as a learner recognises that 'learning is being you', taking us to the heart of what it means to be human and members of communities – local and global. We believe congruence between 'you' and 'your learning identity' offers a foundation to help us effectively navigate this changing world!

OUR PASSION FOR LEARNING

This book reflects our passion for learning.

The initial goal of this book was to share some thoughts around children and learning. But as we wrote and chatted, our ambition grew as we realised that what we were learning from children had much wider application. As you read, we encourage you to reflect on your own lifelong identity as a learner, and how that cuts across whatever age or stage of life you are at.

As we share, we do use 'I' and 'we' (with 'I' without any further clarification relating to me – Sam). It allows us to draw on personal experiences as well as to recognise the contribution to our thinking that colleagues, amazing professionals, parents and, of course, children have made.

As you read, we want you to be aware that you do make a difference and that every interaction is an opportunity to bring about change in yourself as well as others. So, as well as offering the theory behind our ideas, we have suggested ways in which you can start to explore and extend these in your own practice. Throughout we have included sections labelled 'extending the conversation' with additional questions, references and thoughts to deepen the dialogue around the issues raised. We want you to advance even more effective ways of creating a culture where *all* are aware that learning is allowed.

IT'S TIME FOR A CHANGE

This book does not presume to have all the answers; we want to spark discussions that advance the way in which you approach what it means to be a learner for yourself and those you learn with.

As a response to the coming chapters, we want to start many conversations with you by:

– challenging existing assumptions,

– questioning current practice,

– theorising developing arguments,

– hypothesising on making new connections,

– putting forward ideas on alternative engagement.

Aside from suggesting, proposing, presupposing and presuming, we want to 'postulate', by sharing with you our belief for learning as a basis to drive the conversation and to extend our shared understanding.

> *We want learning to be allowed when ever, who ever, where ever we are - no ages or stages - creating positive learning identities and enduring connections to navigate our changing world.*

We question the existing modus operandi (MO) for learning that contributes little to social capital or individual happiness and is creating a disconnection between how we see ourselves as learners and our capacity to learn. We take a position that allows us to challenge out-of-date assumptions that are still determining how we approach learning, whatever the age and whatever the stage we are at.

We want you to think about assumptions that dominate, that limit and that lead to learners being defined in terms of what they lack or can't do, and stagnant practice fixed by old-fashioned approaches defined by stages of development often correlating to age. We want you to re-imagine, change your practice and use language that celebrates the joy that emanates from a realisation of our innate ability to learn.

We are all a resource for the world. We need to be positive about our ability to learn and help others to do the same. We want you to speak up, influence and make a difference. Most importantly we need to be fully equipped to navigate through complexity, cope with a fluctuating geopolitical landscape, tackle the 'its too hard to do' boxes around issues such as social media and get to grips with the unsolvable – the wicked problems.

Geo-political Landscape – The Growth of Authoritarianism

At the time of writing in 2023 we are at another crossroads. 'Post-truth is pre-fascism' writes Snyder (2019) in his book *Road to Unfreedom*. He explains how toxic ideas, autocratic power and 'fake news' spread from Russia into Ukraine, Western Europe and now to the United Kingdom and the White House. 'Magical thinking', and the open embrace of contradiction is causing many to draw on '1984' analogies. In Orwell's (1949) novel, much of the world is in perpetual war. The United Kingdom is part of a totalitarian superstate, led by Big Brother. It is through policing thought and an oversized PR machinery that a dictatorship is reinforced, constantly undermining history and the value given to independent thinking.

'1984' is fiction, but increasingly world events are inviting us to question where we are headed and how a rise in authoritarianism might be countered by a greater investment in the capacity of the individual to manage data and to draw balanced conclusions. It requires skills and strategies to...

- search and retrieve information from a variety of sources,
- explain concepts in different ways,
- link ideas together and identify sources,
- connect learning from across a variety of experiences.

In other words become and apply connected learning.

Social Media and Mental Health

Another pervasive set of challenges are the issues we face around mental health and its association with the part social media plays in many of our lives. Only recently MSBNC broadcast the legal efforts of a US school board who were taking social media companies to court in search of damages for alleged harm to children's mental health (MSBNC, 2023). This follows a growing sense of the risks social media poses to society (Haidt, 31/7/21). Jean Twenge's book *Generation Me: Why Today's Young Americans Are More Confident, Assertive, Entitled and More Miserable* (2006) encapsulates the challenge. The interactivity of social media pages – 'like' on Facebook, 'retweet' on Twitter and the right and left swipe of dating sites like Tinder – emphasises an online environment where we are constantly comparing ourselves to others. This stress on our emotions demands deeper understanding. A more recent collaboration between Twenge and a team of academics highlights a correlation between smartphone ownership dating from 2012 (2012 marked the year that the majority of Americans owned a smartphone) and higher rates of teenage depression, loneliness, self-harm and suicide. There is a broader global impact for learning in schools, as reflected in relation to PISA (The Programme for International Student Assessment) scores...

> *School loneliness increased 2012–2018 in 36 out of 37 countries. Worldwide, nearly twice as many adolescents in 2018 (vs. 2012) had elevated levels of school loneliness...The psychological well-being of adolescents around the world began to decline after 2012, in conjunction with the rise of smartphone access and*

increased internet use, though causation cannot be proven and more years of data will provide a more complete picture.

(Twenge et al., 2021, p. 257)

Our assessment here is not on the place of social media in our lives, but more on the way in which we as humans are able to manage it. It is this capacity to be able to notice, make sense and then navigate the challenge that requires us to re-imagine what it means to be a learner.

Wicked Problems

The nature of the local and global challenges we face can be characterised as 'tame' or 'wicked' problems. Tame problems can be solved by following a linear 'waterfall' process of resolution, as outlined in Fig. 1.

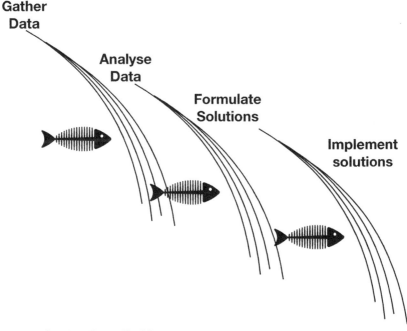

Fig. 1. Solving Tame Problems.

However, as soon as problems become complex, the 'waterfall' process, with a focus on data collection to drive 'solutions', becomes inoperable.

'Wicked problems' (Rittel & Webber, 1973) are a class of dynamic and evolving problems with no obvious identifiable solution, involving multiple stakeholders who may have conflicting interests and are managing contradictory evidence.

They are characterised by not having a set number of potential solutions, due to the fact that each problem is essentially unique. As a result, wicked problems can be interlinked and a symptom of other problems, meaning that there can often be more than one explanation. The result,

– *no definitive formula* to get to a solution

– *incomplete factors and complex interdependencies* as the norm

– *no stopping rule* – there's no way to know your solution is final

– *every attempt counts significantly* – there's no opportunity to learn by trial-and-error

(See Rittel & Webber, 1973)

Global Warming, an Example of a Wicked Problem

Global warming is a wicked problem with no obvious solution. It is unique and has been talked about since the 1980s. It is difficult to solve, whether or not it is impossible to solve, we have to hope. It is an example of incomplete data factors, with a lack of reliable information about how much any country has reduced its CO_2 emissions. The scientific consensus that the climate is warming and this is being caused by humans is not subject to contradictory evidence to any significant degree – 'the scientific consensus that humans are altering the climate has passed 99.9%' (Guardian 19/10/2021); however, there is contradictory evidence regarding potential solutions, the pros and cons of nuclear energy, for example. Nations contain multiple stakeholders with different agendas and interests, political parties, lobby groups, think-tanks and big business.

THE CASE FOR CONNECTED LEARNERS

We would argue that learning from experience is dependent upon the ability to understand how to learn and that only through an explicit understanding of how to connect our learning can each of us advance our learning capabilities. Navigating the geo-political landscape, rise of globalised communication and social media, mental well-being and interconnected wicked problems, bring additional contradictions for us to resolve and with it more need for an approach to face these challenges with well-informed hope.

For us, that hope takes root in the connected learner, with an ability to make connections between the world we live in and our own sense of self. We do not live or learn in a vacuum, by making visible the social context for learning; we are more readily able to understand our capability as a learner. It is a desire to (re)ignite a passion to be a learner that provides the opportunities for us to advance our knowledge, skills and strategies to manage the complexities of the issues we face in our communities and beyond.

Extending the Conversation

(1) This was our first stab at "What is Learning Allowed?" pull it apart and develop further.

Learning Allowed

enabling positive learning identities,
through realising our capacity as 'connected learners'

as we embrace 'learning is being you' – explored through the myriad of spaces and interactions that we encounter in our everyday lives, maximising learner potential through increasing the visibility of the different dimensions of a learning experience and enabling individuals to effectively navigate a changing world.

(2) The following quote highlight the complicated nature of the social world we are part of, explore this in the context of some of the social pressures noted above – what would you add?

...we human beings live and think in immensely complicated social settings that have emerged from the uncoordinated choices and actions of billions of people over thousands of years. Emergent phenomena, such as actual languages, religions, governments, and communities, are at the heart of our moral concerns. Although human beings with evolved characteristics have made these institutions, they take on lives of their own and influence us profoundly while also structuring the decisions we make.

(Levine, 8/9/2014)

2

AN APPROACH – TO ALLOWING LEARNING

> ...*in this century our most important skill is our ability to continually learn and this cannot be acquired simply by adding more subjects to the curriculum or making the existing school day more efficient. A different model of education is required.*
>
> *(Cottam, 2018, p. 32)*

We are entering a fourth industrial revolution (World Economic Forum, 2023) that brings the potential for the 'most profound change in human history' (Russell, 2021), with implications for every aspect of our daily lives. Our approach offers a response to this changing social, technological, environmental, health and economic climate by demanding that we re-position learning in our daily consciousness. We promote the need for all of us to be more in tune with our identity as learners, embracing learning as a part of 'being you'. It marks a shift. The art of learning emerges from defined spaces and moments in our life course, and becomes part of our everyday – whoever and wherever we are.

This chapter will introduce the approach to you, in particular our focus on value, voice and vision as markers through which to think about our identities as learners. An overview is shared below.

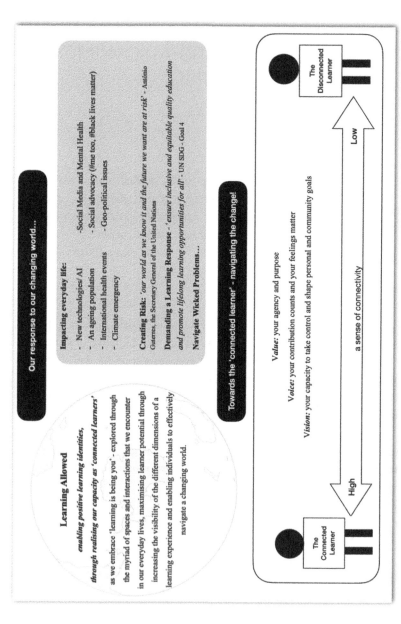

Fig. 2. Responding to Our Changing World.

The speed and reach that current global change, as reflected in Fig. 2, is having on people's everyday lives, is unprecedented (Fig. 3).

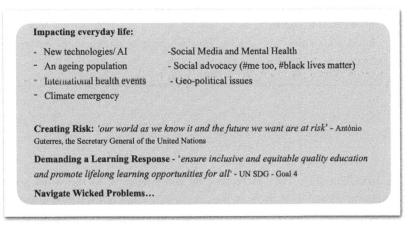

Fig. 3. Global Influences and Impacts.

Such is the profound nature of this change that the UN Secretary General has signalled the threat that we face, 'our world as we know it and the future that we want are at risk' (UN, 2019). It is a statement that demands a response.

In order to mitigate this risk, the UN have set themselves 17 Sustainable Development Goals (UN, 2023). Goal 4 is – '[to] ensure inclusive and equitable quality education and promote lifelong learning opportunities for all' (Goal 4, UNSDG). This recognises learning must be part of a solution to enable positive global change.

However, to implement certain fundamental questions must be addressed.

– Who is a learner (does 'all' really mean all)?

– What is learning for (what is the purpose of those opportunities)?

– How can we allow learning (what does an equitable and quality education look like)?

Once we start to interrogate these questions we realise that for Goal 4 to be more than a statement of purpose, it requires us to commit to learning and the learner in a radically different way. It is by engaging with these questions that our ambitions for 'Learning Allowed' become clear. We position this approach as a shift from where we are to where we need to be. The three following chapters will set out this transition – illustrating the paradigm shift that is required. We will mark an awareness of two opposing ends of a scale, one marked by learner connection, the other by disconnection. Establishing a resilient and ever present learning identity built on a sense of our connection as learners is, we would suggest, key to our ability to navigate this changing world successfully.

> **Extending the Conversation**
>
> Using our diagram 'Fig. 2 – responding to our changing world', discuss with others and add to it.
>
> Build your vision and discuss how learning to navigate our present and future is crucial for all of us.

THE CONNECTED LEARNER – CREATING A POSITIVE LEARNING IDENTITY

Our paradigm shift seeks to re-position the learner in (i) the wider social consciousness and (ii) in the way we see ourselves and our learning potential. Over the coming chapters, we will build up our awareness of what influences our learning identity, as we draw attention to:

- Learning as a lifelong journey
- Connectivity as a sense of value, voice and vision
- Identifying and controlling disconnection
- The fluid nature of our learning identities – the connection continuum

LEARNING IS A LIFELONG JOURNEY

One of the challenges that we have with 'learning' is the way in which it is associated with particular moments in the life course, for example between the ages of 5 years and 16+, many of us go to school.

One of the early conversations Caroline and I had was learning about learning from children had significant application for others, whatever their age. Caroline, in passing, suggested we should be thinking about our 'seven ages of learning'. It was a reference to Shakespeare's 7 ages of man. I could just about remember them, but a quick internet search on the monologue delivered by Jaques in As You Like It – beginning 'all the world's a stage...' (Shakespeare, 2005) confirmed that we had... (Fig. 4).

An Approach – To Allowing Learning

1	Infancy
2	Primary age
3	Secondary age/ teenager
4	Young adult
5	Middle age
6	Old(er) age
7	Advanced years/ End of life

Fig. 4. The Seven Ages of Learning.

Presenting certain 'ages' can universalise members of a group, fixing them to a particular stage, with certain requisite capabilities; it can also enable us to view learning as something that happens across time. Learning must be seen as lifelong, which by recognising as a journey allows us to…

– situate all individuals as a 'lifelong connected learner',

– demonstrate the connectivity between an individual's learning knowledge, strategies and skills in one stage and apply to another,

– recognise the positive and negative learning experiences that we all pull through as threads across lives,

– emphasise that learning is 'who we are' not limited to specific learning programmes or spaces. There is value in explicitly 'connecting learning' an individual learning experiences across different settings and different times.

Acknowledging these 'seven ages' as an illustration of a learning journey throughout our lives, we get the chance to explore and investigate the myriad of connections that makes learning part of who we are. It is that desire to see learning as a reflection of our wider identity as humans, that defines our ambition for all to know that 'Learning is Allowed'.

CONNECTEDNESS IS AN AWARENESS
OF YOUR VALUE, VOICE AND VISION

To learn our way through the global changes that we face demands that we recognise we have an innate capacity to learn. However, to make full use of this ability, we have to have a way of assessing our individual learning proficiency and attitudes both in respect of what enables and limits us. We introduce 'value, voice and vision' as filters for self-analysis. Growing through a personal awareness of our connectedness allows us to challenge our limitations and transfer and build on our successes so expanding the possibilities of what it means for us to be a learner (Fig. 5).

Fig. 5. Connectivity Continuum.

Meet Jack – Case Study

> *I (Sam) first met Jack in the headteachers office. He had been sent there for being disruptive. This was not his first visit. Jack was making this solo trip between the classroom and office on an almost daily basis. He was matter of fact in his interview with the head teacher, resigned to whatever he was 'told' to do next. It was clear that although Jack was physically present, he was emotionally absent. Jack was a disconnected learner.*
>
> *Of course I had seen children disconnected in school before, but here the level of disconnection was extreme. Jack seemed to revel in it. Indeed, it was clear that this indifference was part of who Jack sought to portray himself as. In Jack's mind, the more overt the disconnection demonstrated, the more this fuelled his social capital, his status. At school, Jack had decided to play this part, which could be displayed best by rejecting the expectations set by adults and actively sabotaging his own learning. In short, Jack had created an identity for himself as a non-learner.*

In the weeks that followed, Jack gave us a crucial insight into his experiences of 'learning' (creating a foundation for the research that followed). We talked about his feelings, and the relevance of activities in the classroom, as well as power, relationships, ambition and motivation. From rocket images to support Jack manage his feelings to riding his BMX bike in the playground, we explored what it meant for Jack to envisage himself as a learner.

My conversations with Jack centred on three recurring themes:

- Value
- Voice
- Vision

Value: The idea of the 'emotional bank account' kept coming to mind in my early meetings with Jack. In an emotional bank account – a positive comment about one's character or actions count as credits and negative comments as debits. In a school context, I wondered how the emotional bank account might be used to give children a way to think about themselves as learners. A positive comment on an aspect of learning = credit and a comment or action that results in questioning their learning capacity = debit. With Jack, the activity in his bank account was debit after debit. He found himself continually in conflict with teachers and other children; his behaviour was subject to repeated words or actions that emphasised his learning failures. There was nothing being 'paid in', Jack had no credits, therefore no foundation on which to build any positive sense of himself as a learner. Before Jack and I could even discuss learning, he needed to realise his value, his own capabilities, creating a foundation on which he could then explore what it meant to be a learner.

Voice: As I got to know more about Jack over the coming weeks, it became clear that part of Jack's challenge as a learner was that he had lost or had no voice. Yes, Jack could make a noise in the classroom; yes, he could be dismissive, aggressive (as well as kind), but he did not have any way of using his voice to take control of his learning. The lack of value he had in himself, coupled with a limited vocabulary for sharing his feelings and talking about the processes of learning, added to Jack's sense of being disconnected from learning. As a consequence, Jack found it hard to know which were the right 'pathways' to enable his thoughts and ideas to be shared in a constructive way, often leading to sudden outpourings of emotions. As Jack started to recognise a sense of value in himself, he started to find his voice and use it. Jack increasingly realised how to make a contribution to the learning communities he was part of, offering some sense of control as he struggled to overcome the perceived effect of power on the relationships around him. A realisation of his voice was transformational for Jack.

Vision: Jack's experiences and the resulting perception of himself as a learner were defined by the labels others had given him relating to his background and past behaviours. Jack did not meet the adult expectations associated with the traditional learner; this translated into Jack's lack of motivation and ambition. Jack's belief was that the title of 'learner' should not be attributed to him. Being a learner was for children that followed school rules, who came from stable homes, who could do maths, were good at recognised sports; this was the basis for ambition; this was the foundation on which hopes for the future were based. What did he have to aim for? His sense of identity as a 'non learner' was simply creating a self-defeating spiral of action as he continued to search for opportunities that reinforced an identity of indifference and disconnection, rather than one of hope. Over the next three months Jack began to recognise his value and that he had a voice, he began to explore the vision he had for both his own learning but also the part he could play in the learning community as a whole.

APPLYING OUR MODEL: VALUE, VOICE AND VISION

Jack had given us insight and in the research that followed, value, voice and vision became defining as a means for assessing learning connectedness. The more we shared these concepts, the more we saw how they applied to all learners – they became a focus for making sense of learning identities and offering a route to the 'connected learner'.

OUR VALUE

Our Value: A Sense of Agency and Purpose

Before any individual can discuss their learning, they need to hold value in themselves. It requires a recognition by the individual, a desire to see the learner in terms of their own agency. Acknowledging the agency of the learner, which we define in terms of the individual's capacity as a meaning maker, starts to shift us away from a focus on 'performance' that has determined the way that so many think about their learning identities. This constant internal evaluation around whether 'I am good enough' marks a wider narrative around children's competence that has been a defining feature in their relationship with adults. For the *disconnected learner*, school, in the words of Carol Dweck (2006), is a place where children learn what they 'can do' and what they 'don't know' rather than equipping them to recognise their potential and to explore and discover those skills that allows them to take on what they 'can't do' and what they 'want to know'. Dweck calls this 'growth mindset'. It leads Dweck to the following question, 'is success about learning or proving you're smart?' (2006, p. 16). Responding to this demands that we review our attitudes towards education, is it

(1) a place of limitless possibilities or

(2) a setting defined by fixed records of achievement based on adult centric criteria?

If learning is the latter, then it is about judging 'permanent traits' rather than saying to the child, 'you are a developing person and I am interested in your development' (2006, p. 172). In the context of our approach, it is not only about inviting adults to acknowledge the active learning journey children are on but for children to see this too, enabling them to realise that 'interest in their development' – this journey is not just an area of attention for adults but for themselves as well.

Ken Robinson was clear that our obsession with learning based on performance had resulted in individual talent and potential being too often left undiscovered. In his famous TED talk (Robinson, 2006), which he followed up with a book called 'finding your element' (Robinson & Aronica, 2013), he says of children's potential... 'human resources are like natural resources; they're often buried beneath the surface and you have to make an effort to find them' (Robinson & Aronica, 2013, p. xi). To Robinson, being given the opportunity to 'find your element', created the very foundation, not just for learning but for *being*

> ...*finding your element is vital to understanding who you are and what you're capable of being and doing with your life.*
> (Robinson & Aronica, 2013, p. xi)

Without that 'element', he argues we lack balance, with implications for our jobs, our job retention and our motivation (Robinson & Aronica, 2013). The role of the school and other learning spaces should be to encourage a journey that allows us to find out more about who we are, exploring and examining a wide range of aptitudes in contrast to existing 'systems of education [that] operate on a very narrow view of aptitudes' (p. xi).

School, as Ken Robinson explores in *Creative Schools*, can offer the opportunities that allow the individual to get a stronger sense of their personal value (Robinson & Aronica, 2016, p. 53). He highlights a balance in schools between the cultural, the social and the personal and provides examples of how this is happening in countries like Finland. We note that, although Finland is a small country and largely monocultural, their education system offers some useful glimpses of a meaningful relationship between wider society, communities and the individual. All of this has implications for the way school comes to 'a balanced curriculum, high priority practical/vocational learning, effective teacher training, high discretion to head teachers, a focus on collaboration not competition, efforts to maintain close ties with communities'. All of these have had important and significant impact that 'helps students learn' – as such education becomes about creating the conditions for learning, through investing in relationships. There is a greater sense of the symbiosis of child and adult undertaking a shared learning journey as both are in touch with the 'value' of being a learner (now and for the future). The democratic school movement and approaches that broadly recognise these principles (Fielding & Moss, 2010) offers another example marked out by the intrinsic willingness to accept the value of the individual as a learner with implications for the way in which they are seen as capable of making choices in all areas of their learning from curriculum decisions, attendance, evaluation and self-management (see Robinson & Aronica, 2016).

Advancing – Value

Creating Capabilities to Narrate and Navigate Your Learning Journey – A Work in Progress

Our ability to project possibilities for our learning (a theme in the final chapter) must be recognised as personal, as an extension of our learning identity, an extension of 'our story'. Fred Kiel, in his renowned study with business, 'Return on Character' (2015), talks about the value in a coherent life story.

> *Your life story is the narrative you tell yourself and others that allows you to make sense of your life experiences, from your earliest memories onward. Your life story is your answer to two key questions: who am I, and how did I become the person I am…it is only through reflection that we can pull together a review of our life story…that process helps us to understand the pivotal moments and decisions in our past, their patterns, and how they helped bring us to where we are in the present. (2015, p. 54)*

It is the practical sense in which recognising our own narrative gives us the tools to explore our own value and to chart this, that is of such significance. It is that connection between 'who we are' and 'what you are capable of being and doing with your life' (2013, p. xi), that Ken Robinson notes. Indeed, as a response to disconnections, such as:

- people not interested in work,
- children alienated from education,
- rising number of people taking antidepressants, alcohol and drugs,
- levels of youth suicide.

Robinson is saying that finding 'our element' allows us to establish a positive balance to our lives, which also offers a response to some of these destructive social issues. It is a search that Robinson makes clear is about our capacity to narrate our story as we reflect on that 'inward journey to explore what lies within you and the outward journey to explore opportunities in the world around you' (2013, p. 5). Philosopher and faith leader, Jonathan Sachs (2020), talks of how being part of our own stories means we are a work in progress, as we respond to the ever shifting social contexts that we find ourselves in. It is in this active and determined drive to get to know yourself better – to be able to place ourselves – in our own learning stories that offers an important basis for expanding the possibilities that a learning opportunity presents.

> **Extending the Conversation**
>
> Review learning approaches you are already aware of such as Emilio Reggio (Rinaldi, 2006), Montessori (Frierson, 2022) and Steiner (Lachman, 2007) – how and in what ways do these seek to emphasise the 'value' of the learner?
>
> This is just the briefest of overviews of the importance of the place of 'value' in establishing a connected learning identity, talk through the possibilities it offers.

OUR VOICE

Our Voice – A Realisation That Your Contribution Counts and Your Feelings Matter

By voice we denote the owner's authentic voice, their first person experience, hearing from the person themselves. Voice encourages us to move beyond themes of passivity and to actively recognise the importance of intentional listening and the learner being in the present. It is a capacity to 'discern' and as a result knowingly contribute to your own life story that frames our engagement with voice.

The suppression of 'voice' has been a defining aspect of authoritarian power hierarchies. The controlling of voice has been a feature of societies through the ages, with those at the top 'having a say' over what should be shared and by whom. It is only in recent history that women – half the world's population – have had a voice, and it is a sharp rebuke on our global community that for many women and people of colour, this still remains a dream rather than a reality. Children being seen and not heard is still the norm. Take, for example, the way in which some have responded to the campaigning of Gretta Thunburg, and the efforts to limit or devalue her voice on the basis that she was 'just a child'; notably the then republican President of the United States was one of these critics (Guardian, 24/9/2019). Movements like #MeToo, Black Lives Matters, March for our Lives and

Fridays for the Future have shown the extent to which voices are starting to be recognised though of course there is 'backlash'. Using voice, to be heard and through this advancing understandings of 'hidden' issues, creates an improved basis for more meaningful responses.

It is the same principle for all of us and especially children in their learning. If children's voices are not realised then our ability to support them and equip them to respond to the ups and downs of their learning life journeys is very limited. Later (see Part 2) we look at a 'culture of advocacy' (Frankel, 2018a) as a means to highlight (1) the need to establish the voice of the child (2) to find platforms that allow that voice to be amplified. It is a basis for thinking about children's voice within their learning, not just in relation to any macro activities they might choose to be involved with, climate activism, for example, but also in relation to those micro elements of their day-to-day lives – what to wear and what to eat, though to the strategies they use to explore a learning goal.

A research initiative that captures the transformational impact that children's voices can have on communities, including how they are seen as learners, was a project called The Shinning Recorders of Zisize in South Africa (Children Count). What was so powerful about this research was the way in which it allowed the researchers to not only question but also to present to the wider community, the power hierarchies and assumptions that framed how children were positioned within society. Through giving the children a microphone and inviting them to start conversations with adults in their lives about issues that were relevant to them, adults began to hear children differently. One example was an interview that 10-year-old Mpumelelo conducted with his mother following the selling of his goat. Mpumelelo explains that after a day away from the family home he got back to find the goat had gone and when *I asked them. . .they ignored me*. When he later asked his mother about this – she said *we decided that it was better to sell it and buy you another one*. In response to why he was not told, his Mum said *it's because we felt that you were still young and we didn't think that we needed to tell you*. The brilliance of the project lay in simply enabling these conversations to happen. Through equalising the power through the use of the microphone, Mpumelelo was able to have a conversation he would not otherwise have been able to have, challenging and changing his mother's perceptions and creating a new basis for their relationship. This was summed up by another parent who responded to an interaction with their child (on a different issue) by saying, *I never realised that [you], my child, felt the pain of what we were going through at that time in our lives. I didn't think children were aware of so much that is going on around them* (Meintjes, 2014, p. 162). The foundation that enabling children's voices offered, in relation to promoting positive change, was reflected in the comments of this school principal. . .

> *What I have learnt is that we look at kids or think about kids as not being aware of issues, or of issues not affecting them. But after hearing the programs [the children's recordings] I've realised that children know about things we think the don't know about. I realised that they know, and if given the chance to speak about those things, they speak. I realised that they think deeply about these things and these issues that they raise... I no longer look at children as mere children who do not know anything. I look at them as people who know something and who have something to say to me, and who can speak freely and be just as confident as an adult.*
>
> *(Meintjes, 2014, p. 163)*

It is a powerful extract that highlights the transformational impact of giving children the chance to be part of the conversation, for their voices to be heard.

In the wider context of schools, voice continues to be both challenging and offer opportunities. So many times schools have responded to my questions about children's voice with – 'well we have a school council'! The problem is that school councils get wheeled out as the pinnacle of adult action in relation to children's voice, rather than a starting point. School councils can be tokenistic, as schools tick *that* box that is children's voice, consequently the activities that children take part in are minimal and inconsequential. There are, however, growing examples of ways in which children's voices are being amplified through expanded participatory frameworks (see Unify your Language – Chapter 8). Notably, that will to establish the voice of the child and then start to amplify it, offer opportunities to re-think trust and power, where children can be involved in the processes of assessment. The image of 'pupil as a professional', exemplified in a report called Inspiring Schools (Davies et al., 2005), creates a platform that allows adults and children to be part of understanding the learning process together, recognising we are 'all' learners. In practice, it enables children and adults to be supported in making greater sense of their learning, through learning conversations that encourage a shared vision for learning in that community.

Advancing – Voice

Creating Capabilities to Amplify Voice – Strengthening Learning Partnerships

An emerging theme in relation to voice is how it can be used to instigate and nurture relationships (we explore this in more detail in Chapter 10). Rights have become a common basis for seeking to define children's voice. John Wall in his book on 'children's rights' talks about a number of reasons why such 'rights' are important. He advances a view that moves rights away from being an 'entitlement' to become a focus for guiding social collaboration and group enfranchisement, which as a consequence enables deeper conversations about a shared humanity and being part of a more just society. Using rights as a means to challenge existing areas of disconnection caused by inequality and an abuse of power, he emphasises the need for rights to be seen as a means to 'empower persons in diverse ways as interdependent members of society' (Wall, 2016, p. 159). It is that need for empowerment within the context of interdependent relationships that offers such an important model for learning communities (Correia, 2023).

However, this requires that both children and adults, learners and facilitators, see the importance of relationships as a means to build and further their sense of voice and through this strive for a shared community of practice built on a unified ambition for a 'common' good, which we expand on in the discussion on 'vision' below.

Our approach to voice extends the conversation beyond an assumption that the adult knows best, moving us away from speaking on behalf of a group. A powerful example of this is shown in the work on child abuse, which highlights the need to break taboos and enable children's voices to be heard. The work of Jenny Kirtzinger has shown that the traditional adult centric response has been (and often remains) one dimensional, however, by establishing the voice of the child, and offering them a platform to talk on this issue, it created a basis for more informed understanding of the way in which children were seeking to make sense of these terrible experiences. As a result of enabling the voice of the child, a conversation emerges that is more focused on 'oppression' rather than 'vulnerability' and 'liberation' rather than 'protection' (Kirtzinger, 2010, p. 433), offering a foundation to build partnerships that can drive systemic change.

Extending the Conversation

Today voice is a powerful commodity, illustrated in the way it might be used to amplify an idea or a position. Voice here is not a campaign to turn everyone into a global activist, but for us all to see the worth in our own individual voice and the voice of others.

What do you understand by voice and how and why is it relevant for learners in your learning community?

In the context of an era of 'post truth', how does a focus on voice better equip us to know our voice and to use it?

OUR VISION

Our Vision – Awareness of Your Capacity to Take Control of Your Learning Journey, Shaping Ambitions for Yourself and Your Community

A defining feature of many learners experiences is how they are shaped by the labels that others attach to them and their learning. As we internalise this, the result is often a narrowing of the pathways that we see as options within our learning journeys. 'Vision' invites the learner to recognise their enormous capabilities to search for the right possibilities that allows them to extend their learning experiences, maximising opportunities within the context of their individual learning goals and ambitions.

Change is marked by 'movement…metamorphosis or transformation…the appearance of new characteristics' (Patterson, 2018, p. 13). The sense of vision which we are trying to convey to you here is children (or learners) can be part of *their* process of change. As a starting point, it requires a recognition of being a change makers, overcoming perceptions of the power relationships that have traditionally dominated children's lives. As we think about the role of children in relation to change, it invites us to reflect on 'why teachers don't teach students how to be powerful' (Shutz & Sandy, 2011, p. 14). This raises important questions that have application across those spaces that adults and children share. As we think about vision, we are also thinking about how to re-cast these relationships in a way that brings people together. This has been illustrated in international development work that has seen a shift from the imposition of ideas, to community, and indeed child-led initiatives (See Chapter 9 – Meaningful Opportunities).

In many ways, this is about the need, in our changing world, to re-engage with the vision we have for a 'common good'. The ever reflective Jonathan Sachs (2017), mentioned earlier, spoke about this in his highly watched TED talk, as well as in his final major publication, *Morality* (Sachs, 2020). He questions the society we have become by challenging the cult of 'I', reflected in pop songs and political speeches. Pointing to the rise of mental health issues and the realities of loneliness he draws on the work of Robert Hall, who says 'relationships are the most valuable and value creating resource of any society'. The problem that Sachs notes is that 'in place of *we*, we have been left with *me*', 'the solitary individual whose needs, wants and desires take precedence over the collective' (p. 86). Sacks challenges us to review this egotistical position of the self in light of evidence from business[1] and health (some of which we have already looked at), where a focus on 'we' has positive impacts in relation to happiness, self-worth and productivity. Establishing that sense of a common good – a shared vision – is dependent on mutual relationships. Such relationships, Sachs suggests, demand effort driving a deeper connection as it is 'only when we encounter another human being that we begin to communicate and construct a shared world out of the art of communication' (2020, p. 61). It is that need for adults and children to 'encounter' one another through effective communication that is so relevant in the context of the *connected learning* approach as they form deeper and more meaningful learning relationships. For an encounter demands first, a removal of assumptions; second, an equalising of power; and, third, it asks that we see each other in full, it requires an openness and a vulnerability. That requirement for authenticity should not be underestimated. Indeed, it will only happen when the individual recognises their value, voice and vision in the context of those that they are interacting with.

Enabling children to share in a vision for their communities (whether at home or school)[2] is empowering. It relies on an inner sense of purpose, in which the individual child not only recognises the contribution they can make but also that this is part of them fulfiling their role within that community. Jessica Taft's research on working children's organisations in Chile (2019) explains what happens when children are enabled to hold that sense of vision (both in themselves and for their communities). We are introduced to a state of being that goes beyond mere citizenship to an increasingly embodied recognition of oneself as an activist. This is an over simplification, which is perhaps better summed up in the words of 15-year-old Joaquin, who said

> ...from the beginning of my involvement I knew that kids are capable of doing many things and of contributing to making a better world, a more just world...But I've learned that we are social actors...And more than this, we have to make ourselves part of the public.

---

1 Research highlights the value for business leaders to invest in relationships. As Kiel (2015) notes, successful business increasingly values traits such as – openness, conscientiousness, extroversion, agreeableness, risk aversion/fear.
2 The notion of communities as cultural units (Cohen, 1982) is powerful, as it allows us to think about the multitude of communities that we are a part of.

What Joaquin's words reflect is not only that sense of value and voice but also a deep belief in how this should inform a contribution to society and how these young people should share in a vision for their communities. The term used to describe this is 'protagonisimo', as Taft shares 'protagonisimo is simply recognising the vocation of all social groups to think, suggest and act with their own imagination, their own identity, with the capacity for self determination' (2019, p. 65) (also see – Cussianovich, 2001). Taft reflects on this in terms of it affirming 'children's inner lives [and] their capabilities' (2019, p. 65). That sense of enabling a 'vocation', one that is deeply rooted in one's identity – is part of their inner lives – is precisely what we are seeking to do in relation to learning. Enabling that sense of vision – that inner belief in the value of learning and how as a learner we can be part of shaping a common good with all the possibilities that a truly collaborative iteration of this involves – is not only exciting but also transformative.

Advancing Vision

Creating Capabilities to Identify Pathways That Expand Learning Possibilities

In his first speech after leaving the White House, Barak Obama talked about his vision of supporting young people as future leaders. He talked of their capacity as 'sharp', 'astute', 'tolerant', 'thoughtful' and 'entrepreneurial' and ended with the following question – 'what are the ways in which we can create pathways for them to take leadership, for them to get involved?' (ABC7, 24/4/17). Not only does this reference reflect that desire for children to be a part of shaping communities but it also challenges us to think about the 'how' of participation. There is also a third point it raises. For even if we (adults) create those pathways, do children and young people or adult learners recognise that those pathways are actually open to them? Some of this goes back to a sense of our potential (as noted earlier in relation to value), but it is also about knowing the actual steps that are needed through which one can take control and put one's ambitions into practice. Vision here is not about unfounded dreams; it is about understanding the hope that comes from knowing there are steps you can take to bring a learning vision to life.

What we are pointing to here is even when our destination may be uncertain, we still have to know how to find a path that allows us to pursue our vision. It is from that awareness that we gain a sense of control and are able to effectively pursue our learning possibilities. Notably, that sense of control has been linked to feelings of happiness and satisfaction that then drives our motivation and desire to want to continue the task. In his book *Flow: the Psychology of Happiness*, Csikszentmihalyi talks about the ideal state for learning. The reason this is important is that being in this state has positive, well-being implications – it allows our hugely underused brain to fire (1997). This ideal state for learning is not a relaxed and detached position, but as with a growth mindset it is one where we are managing higher levels of challenge alongside low levels of stress, learning to a sense of satisfaction. It is this that Eric Jensen refers to in Completing the Puzzle, that as we seek to manage the task, and we are able to take and make choices, our brains 'end up in a far better chemical state than when we are told what to do' (cited in Gilbert, 2013, p. 97). Indeed, he argues that this releases those chemicals that produce a sense of 'pleasure'. The point is that there is value in being able to complete the task effectively, not following orders but making our own choices as part of our own efforts to pursue a learning goal.

The sense of hope that this builds creates a positive feedback loop, where our depth of connection fills us with a will to keep on learning. As educationalist Ian Gilbert says,

> *...when we are in a state of hopefulness our brains literally light up with electrical energy coursing around the upper intellectual regions. However, when we find ourselves in a state of hopelessness the brain will dim with the energy downshifting... to the lower, more basic, do the minimum to survive elements. (2013, p. 180)*

The recognition that there are possibilities open to you and there are reasons to be hopeful, re-directs the learner from dark alleys and dead ends to well-lit roads where you have a clear sense of moving forward.

Extending the Conversation

To what extent should learning and the learner be part of shaping community vision for today and tomorrow?

IDENTIFYING DISCONNECTION FROM LEARNING

This focus on value, voice and vision was providing a lens through which to start meaningful conversations about how we perceive ourselves as learners and…a pattern was emerging.

One activity I had started to use when working in a new school was to ask children and adults how they viewed themselves as learners. What stood out from these conversations was that 'being a learner' was conditional. For many adults, their sense of identity as learners appeared to be partial or fleeting; it is something 'we were' for a time rather than 'we are'. Amongst children, being a learner was too often aspirational; it is a goal to be aimed at, precipitating a flood of anxieties over whether those defined targets of success would ever be met. What we were seeing was a variety of barriers that were disconnecting people from seeing themselves as a learner, resulting in them questioning their learning capacity (ability to learn) and their related ambitions and goals.

We would suggest that it is a lack of value, voice and vision that is a constant theme in research that reflects a serious disconnection between children, young people and adults and how they view themselves as being a learner. Over the last 10 years, the Good Childhood Report has been capturing data about children's lives in the United Kingdom. In 2019–2020, the report started to flag a disparity between the way children felt about school in 2009–2010 and then ten years later. In their 2022 report, the Children's Society highlighted themes linked to happiness being lower than a decade ago and that school was a part of life that children felt most unhappy about. Although the findings were not conclusive, themes emerged such as older learners feeling less happy than younger learners with school work and how a sense of being 'listened to' increased happiness – notably – '1 in 5 children did not think they had a say in decisions that were important to them' (p. 44). These findings about the decline in attitudes towards school is reflected in other reports (Organisation for Economic Cooperation and Development, 2019; WHO, 2020) (Fig. 6).

England, Wales and Scotland were among the six countries out of 45 with the highest levels of school work pressures	WHO, 2020
children in the UK had the greatest fear of failure and the lowest life satisfaction' when compared to other European countries.	PISA (Program for International Student Assessment), 2018

Fig. 6. Pressures for Learners.

For those facing disadvantages the challenges are amplified. High levels of inequality, represented by the widening of the attainment gap between children from higher and lower income families (for the first time in 10 years), also leaves those children from less financially stable backgrounds facing particular challenges linked to fatigue and poor concentration (Children and Young People Now, 2022).[3] A worsening of the economic situation in the Autumn of 2022, on top of the pressures to learners created by the COVID-19 pandemic, has created a verifiable cocktail of challenges impacting children's learning experiences, and ultimately how they connect with being a learner.

This is not just a UK problem! That pressure on value, voice and vision is recognised in other reports in other countries. An example from a UNICEF report on school experiences in Canada states

> ...while Canada's schools tend to offer high performing learning environments, they are also high pressure environments and seem to be less successful in fostering children's sense of belonging and well being...
>
> *(UNICEF, 2020)*

Our position is clear, by not engaging with the value, voice and vision of the learner we are simply creating systems that are increasing disconnection by limiting our learning connectivity, reducing and in some cases destroying our association with our inner identity as a learner. This is problematic within the context of a global vision for change that prioritises learning as part of the solution.

LEARNING ALLOWED – A CONNECTION CONTINUUM

As we have reflected above, our identity as learners is affected by a sense of connection and disconnection. Notably, this sense of connectivity is not fixed, but is fluid and changing. It means that we are constantly assessing and re-assessing where we position ourselves on a 'continuum', as illustrated in (Fig. 7).

---

[3] 4.3 million children and young people are in poverty – '9 out of every 30 children is officially poor' – with the result that this group demonstrated fatigue (78%) or poor concentration (75%) at school (NEU Survey, 2021).

An Approach – To Allowing Learning   29

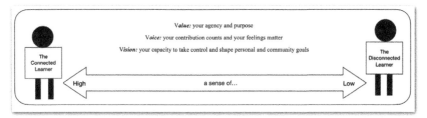

Fig. 7. Connection Continuum.

It is recognising the changeable nature of our identity as learners that we are (i) better placed to support those learners like 'Jack', who not only have a deeply rooted perception of themselves as a 'disconnected learner' but also (ii) to manage the everyday fluctuations, that we all experience, in our learning moods.

> *We will all experience shifting confidence in ourselves as learners depending on the context. It is something we have regularly talked about in the writing of this book. How many times has our sense of identity as a learner shifted as we have waited on a thumbs up from the other, or a word of encouragement to restore our self confidence.*

Our ambition in the coming chapters is to create an awareness of what might influence where we position ourselves on this connection continuum in relation to any learning goal. At the start of this chapter, we set out three questions in response to the UN's SDG 4, which were...

(1) Who is a learner (does 'all' really mean all)?

(2) What is learning for (what is the purpose of those opportunities)?

(3) How can we allow learning (what does an equitable and quality education look like)?

Each question highlights barriers and enablers that influence our sense of value, voice and vision. As we work our way through the coming chapters, our ability to understand what the ingredients of the connected and disconnected learner are will become more defined, allowing us to explicitly identify the changes in approach that we need to make (Fig. 8).

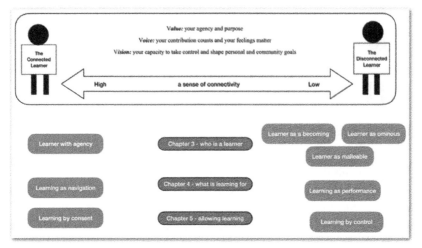

Fig. 8. Influences on Our Sense of Connectivity.

In presenting a model for navigating change, Chris Lever (2018) talks about the importance of us being able to define, 'where we are', 'where we are going' and 'how we are going to get there'. Chapters 3–5 focus on those first two elements, giving us that sense of the learning journeys that we might need to take.

Chapters 6–11 addresses – the 'how' through a reconsideration of practice.

Our goal is to make being a 'connected learner' an achievable ambition for all of us – whoever and wherever we are.

Extending the Conversation

As you reflect on value, voice and vision, what does this mean to you (as a learner and/or as a facilitator/teacher)?

Choose one new thing you want to learn and identify where you position yourself on the connection continuum and why.

THE CONNECTED LEARNER IN THEORY

3

WHO IS A LEARNER?

> ...at the age of six, I gave up what might have been a magnificent career as a painter. I had been disheartened by the failure of my Drawing Number One and my Drawing Number Two. Grown-ups never understand anything by themselves, and it is tiresome for children to be always and forever explaining things to them.
>
> (Saint Expurey, 1943)

At the end of the last chapter – we highlighted our intention to turn a theoretical question, 'who is a learner', into a practical approach that allows us to advance our understanding and create individual positive learning identities.

As we think about 'who is a learner', we begin to see pervasive discourses that continue to dominate understandings and have a deep impact on the way we come to see ourselves and others. The author and journalist David Brooks reviewed the state of the education system in the United States through an examination of 'success'. In his book, the *Social Animal*, he defined a learner as

> ...[someone who was] energetic, honest and dependable. They were persistent after setbacks and acknowledged their mistakes. They possessed enough confidence to take risks and enough integrity to live up to their commitments... they knew how to read people, situations and ideas. The skills the master seamen has to navigate the oceans they had to navigate the world. (2012, p. xiff)

In providing this definition, he was demonstrating that being an effective learner is linked to our capability to draw meanings from social interactions and to act or react to these in positive ways. Learning is characterised by the knowledge, skills and strategies that we develop as well as the relational way in which these are practiced. It is that capacity to assume a social dimension to learning that enables the effective learner, characterised from our perspective by a high sense of value, voice and vision.

Drawing on Brooks' analysis, we present four different perspectives of the learner. Three of these – the learner as a becoming, the learner as ominous and the learner as malleable – have established historical roots and emerge in a range of ways as part of our contemporary understandings of what it is to be a learner. They reflect universal attitudes towards the learner that have limited space for value, voice and vision. We believe these epitomise where we presently are.

Our fourth perspective, the 'learner with agency', results in possibilities that present purpose in a lifetime of investment in value, voice and vision (Fig. 9).

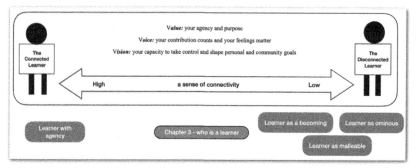

Fig. 9. Chapter 3 Overview.

LEARNER AS A BECOMING

Dominant assumption: learner defined in terms of what they lack and their predetermined future worth

Resulting practice: fixed approaches linked to defined stages of development correlating to age

In the United Kingdom, our curriculum is based on a learner's age and the corresponding stage of their development. This stance can be traced back through the enduring narrative around reason, and the capacity of an individual to process internal thoughts and arrive at considered conclusions. A model of education based around 'reason' has as its first question – 'is this person capable'? It is a premise that results in a focus on what we 'lack' rather than any expectation of ability.

For thinkers like Aristotle, the complete human was a reflection of one's capacity to process information leading to balanced and considered choices.[1] However, the ability to demonstrate rational thought was seen as the purview of only an elite part of society, excluding children and many others.[2] It was within this inner circle of 'power' that learning becomes a means to extend and fulfil one's status and position within society. This is a model where learning is controlled by a single group the 'knowledge holders' who are also the 'knowledge creators'. This interpretation establishes a hierarchy of knowledge, with those at the top of the ladder passing information down to those in the social groups below. Knowledge shared with those with a perceived lack of capacity was not there for challenge or consideration but as pre-packaged 'fact' to be accepted.

Moving into the Enlightenment of the seventeenth Century the capacity to reason was beginning to be extended. John Locke saw the attainment of reason as a journey that the child was on, see Locke (1998). For Locke, learning was a 'progress' in which the individual could draw on a growing set of experiences in order to achieve a desired state of reason, and with it giving society an incentive to establish a broader model of education.

> *[Children are] travellers newly arrived in a strange country, of which they know nothing'. What makes them strangers in our country is their lack of both knowledge and moral sense. Reason covers both aspects of what must be acquired if they are to become full members of our country.*
>
> *(cited in Archard, 2004, p. 3)*

Immanuel Kant suggested that reason was universal and, therefore, could be applied to everyone irrespective of culture or society, with limitations. Children were excluded; women did not carry the same potential to be reasoned thinkers as the educated white male. As Kant was writing for his homogenous academic audience, counter narratives were emerging. For example, former slave Olaudah Equiano was contradicting widely held views that those of African origin were inferior to white people. Equiano demonstrates how white populations ran a successful PR campaign that centred on the need to 'keep them [slaves] in a state of ignorance', seen as 'incapable of

---

[1] From those early recorded thinkers such as Aristotle the notion of reason is a transcendental human quality that extends beyond their physical body. A product of what Aristotle calls 'form' is this ability to reason, which becomes critical to being seen as fully human.

[2] Rational thought for groups like children was seen to be clouded by a focus on emotions – 'they overdo everything, they love too much [and] hate too much'.

learning' as their 'minds are such a barren soil' (1789, p. 110). Mary Wollstonecraft, doyenne of women's rights, talks of society having been taught to see the minds of women as 'enfeebled', with the result that they are treated as 'subordinate beings' (1792, p. 2). As well as gender and race acting as markers for reasoned thought, the evolving presence of compulsory schooling reinforced the place of age as another signifier of competence.

Age as a means of categorisation became even more visible in the 1800s as a result of the emerging 'scientific' study of the child that was encouraged by thinkers such as Charles Darwin. Darwin, in response to his personal curiosity about life, set about observing his own children and exploring a model that linked age to certain moments of human (biological) development (Burman, 1994). This family project created a model of 'normal' biological trajectory as marked by where a child's data sat within quadrants on a graph. This tool had benefits, for example, in relation to health and managing nutrition, but had negative consequences too.[3] A focus on what was 'normal', and more importantly 'who' was normal, had implications for those who did not follow the pattern of the 'norm'. It gave emphasis to the 'value' in grouping children according to certain marked moments, determined by age. Age was used as a universal marker, judgements and assessments could be made for sorting and classifying, with particular implications for children and their learning.

This thinking on biological maturation was extended by those with an interest in the mind, and mental development. As childhood studies academic Sally McNamee highlights, 'certainly within education...developmental psychology became the dominant way of thinking about childhood' (Mcnamee, 2016, p. 29). Indeed it offered a solution to the fears raised by the 'ominous child', as theorists searched for ways to 'produce rational adults out of a mob, mass, or herd...' (Walkerdine, 2009, p. 114). At the heart of this was the work of Jean Piaget.[4] Piaget's research focused on detailed experiments which included giving children a task, such as playing marbles, recording their responses and then creating a series of findings (Piaget, 1935). Piaget's key assertion was children were not capable of abstract thought until they reached the age of 12, with the wider psychological capacities needed for adulthood

---

3 One such consequence can be seen in the developing focus on eugenics. Darwin's cousin Francis Galton became a leading figure in a train of thought around managing those who do not qualify as 'normal'.

4 Although Piaget's work was to be challenged for the way in which it did not acknowledge the social context of children's lives, and the implications this might have for their responses (Donaldson & Hughes, 1979; Donaldson & McGarrigle, 1975), it must also be noted how Piaget did create a focus on children that had not been the case before.

Who Is a Learner?

only developing as they continued to get older. Piaget's model was defined by a number of stages, summed up in brief below:

0–2 years – reflex actions – first motor habits and later sensorimotor activities

2–7 years – initiative behaviour – observable through egocentricity

7–12 years – logic developing – supporting moral and social interaction

12+ years – abstract thinking – ability to offer reasoned judgements.

Piaget's work offered educators a simple model that stressed an association between a particular age and way of thinking about a particular life stage.[5] Curriculum design could be simplified as only certain topics were seen as relevant to children at certain ages. In a powerful piece called *Children's grasp of controversial issues*, Geoffrey Short (1999) reviews the legacy of Piaget. He considers how it was used to preserve views of childhood as a time of innocence, reinforcing the work of thinkers like Jean Jacque Rousseau and Friedrich Froebel.

Short identifies some progress in our view of children, though emphasises that Piaget's ideas are part of the wider context within which we draw our 'image' of the child, specifically shaping those practices that come to be employed in the classroom. With respect to themes such as race, national identity, citizenship and 'controversial issues' in general, Short draws our attention to Piaget's influence calling them[6] moments of 'readiness' that were assigned only when children were seen as capable of engaging in topics. This position is an assumption that continues to influence educators, not only about individual thought but also wider policy such as national curricula. Outdated ideas continue to exert pressure on current practice, as those identified as 'child experts' (Woodhead, 2009), be it teachers, nurses, social workers, continue to make judgements on when children are ready to engage with issues (both in school and beyond). Sex education and raising awareness of LGBTQ+ issues and children's place in such discourse offers very real examples of this rear view thinking being played out today.[7]

---

5 Piaget (1967, p. 3) talks about 'mental life' as a journey towards equilibrium that is represented by the 'adult mind'. Children are moving from a lesser to a higher state of this equilibrium with implications for emotions and wider social relations that are seen to increase with age.

6 See the work of Lawrence Kholberg (1984).

7 The 'Don't Say Gay bill', brought into law by Florida Governor Ron De Santis, provides such an example. This law prevents children from kindergarten to third grade from receiving any teaching around sexual orientation and gender identity (28/3/2022 – Guardian).

> **Extending the Conversation**
>
> An interesting debate that exemplifies the issues around competence is whether children should have the right to vote? How do notions of 'the learner as becoming' restrict children's potential at the ballot box?
>
> John Wall (2016) adds to an examination of 'are children competent to vote?' with the following questions, which you may find interesting to consider. To add to the debate we have added in 'adult' which may enliven the discussion further!
>
> - Are children (adults) sufficiently knowledgeable?
> - Are children (adults) sufficiently independent?
> - Would children's (adult's) voting cause harm to children?
> - Would children's (adult's) voting cause harm to societies?

LEARNER AS OMINOUS

Dominant assumption: learners pose a threat that needs to be controlled

Resulting practice: Surveillance and discipline (through punishment) is demanded to keep control

Virtue sits alongside reason in classical writings, where it is seen as the key accompaniment to an ambition to create a productive adult. However, as Plato and later Aristotle note, virtue education can be applied in different ways and at different levels (Curtis & Boultwood, 1977). Those who will be future law makers must understand the nuances of virtues in a way that was not seen as necessary for those whose role in society required them to follow the 'rules'.[8] Virtue was an area of individual improvement that was regarded as more easily influenced than reason and came to reflect part of daily life, from the pedagogues of classical Greece and Rome who were employed as moral guides to wealthy children (Amos & Laing, 1979) to the pastor in sixteenth century

---

8 Aristotle separates goodness of intellect and goodness of character. Only a few demonstrate goodness of intellect, with a full capacity to reason, whereas all can obtain goodness of character (Burnyeat, 1980).

Europe demanding that parents 'teach' their children to fight an enduring battle against 'original sin'.[9]

This obsession with virtue and character formation can be seen as a 'selling point' in early schools and is a key part of the birth of compulsory schooling. The home had been seen as the source of moral instruction, but as the population grew in the eighteenth and nineteenth century, so did the need for the state to control what was seen as a growing threat. This threat was reflected in the media's characterisation of groups of young people[10], and in literary representations like Charles Dickens – Jack Dawkins – the 'Artful Dodger'. The middle classes, already comfortable in the towns, found the new urban poor on their doorsteps. Compulsory schooling offered a means to manage this threat, and to use it as an opportunity to instruct children so that they might become rule abiding adults. School was regarded as a means to maintain social order, to preserve existing hierarchies and ensure each individual was kept in their place. Compulsory schooling becomes the vehicle to give moral instructions, ensuring the populace become compliant future citizens.[11]

> *The lower classes ought to be educated to discharge the duties cast upon them. They should be educated that they appreciate and defer to a higher cultivation when they meet it, and the higher classes ought to be educated in a very different manner, in order that they exhibit to the lower classes that higher education to which, if they were shown to them, they would bow down and defer.*
> (UK Education Secretary in 1867, Robert Lowe see Cockburn, 2013, pp. 94–95)

The desire to 'divide and rule' remains relevant when we think about the implications for those facing disadvantages and about the language of learning and learner with different perceptions depending on social and economic status.

---

9 An example of this might be the *Book of Discipline* – a treatise put together by John Knox and others in the Scottish church in 1561 (Smout, 1969). Notably it made 'school' the third tier in the hierarchy of social framework for virtue education, behind the state and the church.

10 See Pearson (1983).

11 *The Board of Education* 1906 Handbook states – 'the purpose of public elementary school is to form and strengthen character' (Arthur, 2010, p. 37).

Corporal Punishment

The link between learning, morality and the part the individual plays in preserving a 'common good' goes back to Plato. Disciplinary practices from moral teaching in the form of a good example or a guide to the need for punitively controlling the body became a feature in the sixteenth and seventeenth centuries as Puritan thinking prioritised the use of harsh corporal punishment as a means to teach the child. Adults battled to overcome the child's inherent evil.[12] Directed by the church, parents were encouraged to use force to ensure that this evil was effectively 'scourged', as one fifteenth century writer directs 'parents should regard their children as like a young colt, wanton and foolish till he be broken by education and correction' (Fletcher, 2008, p. 3).

Punishment became a core feature of schooling; violence, for example, in public schools was believed to create the type of people that the country needed. As historian Anthony Fletcher highlights these schools 'sold' themselves on producing the kind of people who would

> ...rule England in Parish, county and nation and who would rule the Empire besides, these schools became the front line of English patriarchy. They were men's foremost instrument of the maintenance of class and masculine hegemony. Their importance in the story of boyhood experience between 1600 and 1914 is therefore incalculable.
>
> *(Fletcher, 2008, p. 196)*

Harsh discipline as a means to manage the threat of the child was pervasive, throughout the evolving education system, from the characterisation of Charles Dickens' Wackford Squeers, to the diary of a German teacher who calculated that during his career he delivered 911,572 strokes with a stick, 124,000 lashes with a whip, 136,715 slaps on the hand and 1,115,800 (de Mause, 1974); violence at school was a routine part of children's experiences boxes of the ear.

---

[12] This association with evil, deeply rooted in faith-based understandings, was a very real way of thinking about children that defined adult practices.

Popular twentieth century works such as William Golding's Lord of the Flies, which mirrored psychological experiments that were being conducted around the same time,[13] reflected this level of concern and the dangerous threat posed by the child who was not effectively supervised. This narrative sat alongside the continued use of corporal punishment in schools, banned in schools in the United Kingdom in 1986. It was not until 1998, in England and Wales (later in other parts of the United Kingdom), that legislation ensured the same protection in private schools. Corporal punishment is still legal in some independent school settings that offer part time education in the United Kingdom (End Violence Against Children, 2022); 134 countries still have not prohibited corporal punishment, 1 in 2 of all 6–17-year olds were educated in settings that had legal recourse to violence as part of their approach to learning (Global Partnership to End Violence Against Children, 2021).

Virtue education and how this relates to the place of 'citizenship' in the curriculum[14] does have an important place in school. We return to this in Chapter 5. However, our ability to establish more progressive practice does demand an awareness of the context within which a narrative around 'virtue' has been dominated by a desire to control the 'ominous' learner and to command obedience.

> **Extending the Conversation**
>
> What are the implications for an education system in which there is talk about a 'school-to-prison' pipeline?[15]
>
> Although this is a more explicit topic of debate in the US school system (King et al., 2018), it is also talked about in the United Kingdom (Guardian 18/2/2023). This reference to prison, as well as including important systematic questions around disadvantage and opportunities that lead from failures at school to incarceration, also includes the increased surveillance and punitive approaches taken within schools themselves – such that they become 'environments that resemble prisons' (see King et al., 2018, p. 269). However, recent news stories in the
>
> *(Continued)*

---

13 Reflected perhaps most widely in William Golding's Lord of the Flies, these ideas represented an area of psychological enquiry. Indeed, Golding himself developed the book based on his own observations as a teacher. The point is that it remains hard to escape from the perception that children are a threat and that threat needs to be controlled as we move to the present day. For more see – Perry, 2018.

14 For more on this see Cockburn 2013.

> United Kingdom around searches in schools (Guardian, 13/7/22) or toilet bans add to a narrative around the way in which the school estate is monitored, with implications for how school is perceived – a place of learning or control?
> We return to this in Chapter 5.

LEARNER AS MALLEABLE

Dominant assumption: learners are passive, malleable to adult intervention

Resulting practice: structured adult centric actions create the 'right' environment for shaping productive adults

John Locke's interpretation of children was as a 'tabula rasa' – a blank slate. Society has a responsibility to shape the child and mould them into what they need them to be. The 'normal' child is created by exposing that child to the 'right' kind of social environment (social structures). It is a way of thinking that is a strong feature of sociological thought, particularly the ideas of Emile Durkheim. Durkheim argued that the ongoing nature of society was driven by the exposure that an individual had to the right kind of social forces, particularly the social institutions of which they were a part (home and school, for example).

At the end of the 1800s, the birth of 'sociology' marked a desire to understand how communities functioned through examining the relationship between those structures of society (institutions, governance) and individual behaviours. Emile Durkheim examined this through his well-known studies on suicide, as he explored the 'connections' people had to society. He created a model for making sense of the forces that inform and shape the way an individual comes to act and make choices (Durkheim, 1951). Central to Durkheim's thinking was 'social structure', a concept from which the discipline of sociology is seen to proceed (Jenks, 1996, p. 34). To make sense of the 'rules' that govern social interaction, Durkheim focused attention on 'forces' generated through social structure that drive the transmission of desired 'norms' to an individual. It is a model in which 'structure' is pre-eminent, presuming that if society is structured correctly then the individual would

---

15 See Guardian 18/2/2023

receive, and also effectively transmit, those commonly held values that maintain a harmonious society.

Durkheim's model ascribes a passive role to the individual. The individual is like a piece of technical hardware, waiting to be provided with the appropriate software which will then define its operating scope. For children, Durkheim's (1978) view of socialisation became a focus through which to understand their place in society. Talcott Parsons developed this. For Parsons (1951), socialisation was another means to balance that unpredictability of the child such that the '[child's] volatility is stabilised, its [the child's] riotousness quelled' (Jenks, 1996, p. 13). Through effective socialisation children are 'inculcated' into society; through the exposure to the 'right' social forces children absorb what they need to know, 'learning' from the institutions that society has created. This process of learning was not seen to involve any form of self-reflection, rather learning was strongly linked to 'habit formation' (James, 2013).[16]

This perspective had implications for the way in which homes and schools, for example, were respected as spaces of 'learning'. Within both, children were seen as passive, awaiting the right stimulus to acquire an understanding of societal expectations that would ultimately allow them to fulfil their place in society.

In reflecting on socialisation, Allison James highlights the real dangers of having a view of the child that is defined by their passivity and an 'inherent plasticity of nature' (2013, p. 136). This view assumes the child as a project – moulded into whatever the adult needs them to be, but it also suggests that, through 'school', they can be remodelled if something is found to be out of place/incorrect/objectionable. James suggests that in the face of a social challenge, we can too easily believe that one can 'pop the education pill and all will be well' (James, 2013). Implementing a universal intervention oversimplifies any problem, not recognising the social realities and complexities of children's everyday lives.[17] James invites us to reject traditional socialisation models and their view of children as passive and be more aware of the impact that universal interventions can have on the routine and relationships of individual

---

16 Works on socialisation, such as Elkin's *The Child and Society* (1960), offer arguments that are decidedly tentative about the child's ability to be reflective. To 'learn' was a one way process that through individual exposure to the right forces allowed them to recognise 'patterns, symbols, expectations and feelings of the surrounding world' (Elkin, 1960, p. 5).

17 For example, as James (2013) discusses, it might be the case that educational goals may be more limited in areas of greater disadvantage; however, that doesn't mean that aspirations will be limited for all children who live there.

children's lives. A one dimensional view of the 'education pill' and its reliance on the *learner as malleable* does little to advance our understanding both of children and whatever challenge is being addressed.

> **Extending the Conversation**
>
> Is school the best place for children to learn?
>
> What has been learnt from our experiences of learning during lockdown?
>
> How and in what ways does our experiences of learning during the pandemic continue to inform practice today? See – EquippingKids (2022) https://www.equippingkids.org/media-hub-area/research-briefing-exploring-learning-at-home-school/- what are your thoughts?

LEARNER WITH AGENCY

A New Paradigm

Learner: active meaning maker

Learning: creating knowledge by making sense of our experiences

To move along a continuum from 'disconnected' to 'connected' learner we have to recognise the blocks, the barriers that continue to be present. It is easy to fall into certain ways of thinking about the learner, for example, the 'hard to reach' learner that frequently appears in the tabloid press. However, it is important to recognise that there are other ways of thinking about the learner, ways that do not limit value, voice and vision, but champion them.

Anthropology (amongst other disciplines) in the 1970s was asking questions about the 'mechanistic man' and the limitations it placed on our ability to fully understand the process of meaning making. It reflected a shift away from the ideas of Durkheim and others, previously discussed, as it recognised the importance of the individual's social life as part of how we create and negotiate meanings. The individual emerges as 'convention making' and 'theory constructing' rather than a passive receiver, responding to the natural and social forces that we are surrounded by. Malcolm Crick (1976) looks at the relationship between language and meaning, and how this particular focus on the individual offers new dimensions for understanding. He uses psychological models, such as B.F. Skinner, as a point of comparison. Crick notes how Skinner pursues particular methods, such as 'stimulus-response' as a means of showing how his work is scientific. However, Crick argues that actually it is by engaging with the social dimension 'the anthropomorphic model of man' (89) that brings a stronger position to present more valid findings. For example, in relation to Piaget's work, which we have already discussed, an awareness to advance the research beyond the confines of the laboratory and engage with methodologies that related more directly to children lives – changed the findings because 'the real child's experience within specific social contexts' was recognised (Light, 1986, p. 185).

External and internal, biological or psychological forces are a part of human life, but these alone do not provide a neat thread of causality to an individual's actions and behaviours.

An action or reaction combines

external forces + individual response

It is in this '+ individual response' that we can explore the capacity for individual agency. Antony Giddens (1979) wove both the role of structure and individual agency together. Rather than being defined by structure, what Giddens sets out is a relationship between the individual and the social settings they find themselves in as a process of interaction, where the individual is drawing on that structure and responding to it, creating meanings that are individually distinct as a result of their own experiences.[18] What is emerging is the learner, as highlighted by Crick, with a positive learning identity, that is active and engaged, creating ways of thinking and being that are not pre-defined for them.

RE-IMAGINING THE CHILD

This shift in thought around the 'individual' was to have dramatic implications for reframing societies' approach to children, with real implications for how we think about the learner. From a body of work that was emerging in the 1970s,[19] magnified by the year of the child in 1979, these theoretical stirrings sought to give credence to children's voice, opening a window into children's lives. In stark contrast to the traditional passive view society had held, this

---

18 see Bourdieu 1977.
19 For example, the work of Myra Bluebond-Langner (1978).

movement highlighted their active and involved social ability. The growing body of research demonstrated (as the New Sociology of Childhood – later Childhood Studies[20]) that actual knowledge of children's worlds was extremely limited, shaped by assumptions adults held rather than informed knowledge of children's everyday lives. The lack of child-centred interaction in research had given us at best partial understandings of the child in wider social narratives (including learning), emphasising the disparity between adult interpretations of children and children's lived everyday experiences.

This work around the children and childhood created theoretical building blocks, which included...

(1) *The context for children's experiences:* 'childhood is understood as socially constructed' (James & Prout, 1997, p. 8) – making this visible allows us to see beyond childhood as a defined or fixed period of the life course, which is universal and repeatable for 'all' children. Rather, we begin to recognise the different 'contexts' of children's experiences and the way in which different cultures, for example, might shape or inform a 'childhood'.

   a. Childhoods: recognising the multiple contexts of children's lives and the uniqueness of their experiences,

   b. Dominant Attitudes: ways of thinking about the child (within a defined community) that fuel policy and practice and create perceived expectations for what 'childhood' should be like.

(2) *The competence of the child:* 'Children are and must be seen as active in the construction and determination of their own social lives, the lives of those around them and the societies in which they live' (James & Prout, 1997, p. 8). Our ability to understand children is advanced through acknowledging their capacity as meaning makers, rather than seeing them as passive recipients, 'objects' shaped by social forces they have no control over. Research designed to enable children's participation offers insight where children can be more actively involved in sharing their experiences of their daily lives.

On the basis of these principles – a 'new paradigm' for understanding the child emerges, with profound implications for extending the way we think about the child as learner.

---

20 See discipline defining works – James and Prout (1997) and James et al. (1998) or overviews such as Mayall (2002) and McNamee (2016).

ACKNOWLEDGING THE MEANING MAKER

We have so far highlighted certain discourse and noted the limited learning identities and implications for learner connectivity, reflected in the presence and impact of out-dated constructed understandings.

We now examine children in terms of their 'competence' and their capacity to make meanings, a recognition of agency, allowing us to extend our thinking of the individual (Fig. 10).

Thinking in this way takes us from

i. A model of the individual as a product of their society, as represented by the one directional arrow to

ii. a model where the individual is actively involved in making sense of the world around them, forming a basis for action or reaction.

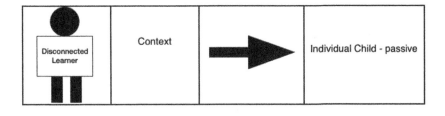

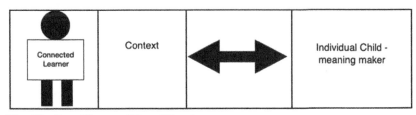

Fig. 10. One-Way and Two-Way Arrows.

The two-way arrow demands a greater awareness of context and making meaning. Adrian James (2010) introduces 'fabric' as a metaphor for thinking about childhood – with weft (the strong threads that run length ways) and the warp (the weave the runs across). In his model, the weft becomes those social forces that set childhood apart (for example, culture, relationships between generations) and the weft is the unique elements of a child's life (their particular interactions). Our interest is in those points of intersection, where meaning comes to be made, as the individual draws from that wider context, enabling a process of meaning making.

In an educational context, this perspective allows us to acknowledge the place of those discourses that are deeply embedded, for example, the 'learner as a becoming' and that focus on ages and stages and examine how these inform the individual as a social agent. It enables us to constructively engage with these discourses, not as singular principles that define practice, but as part of a wider landscape of understanding...

> *To engage with such age based distinctions, which vary from culture to culture, does not mean that we must accede to the influence of developmentalism; however, to ignore reality of such distinctions by seeking theoretical refuge in the singularity thesis would be to side step a major theoretical challenge that clearly faces childhood studies, indeed we must move beyond competing theoretical positions and engage in the task of developing a conceptual framework that will enable the integration of what are, all too often, presented as oppositional perspectives.*
>
> (James, 2010, p. 491)

By adopting this thinking, we can look for links across perspectives and consider how they come to be prioritised and the impact this has on children's experiences. For example, focusing more heavily on children as meaning makers, as we are doing here, does not mean we ignore developmental theories. Rather it allows us to consider the way in which these theories inform the way in which the learner sees themselves, and how that impacts their levels of value, voice and vision.

James' 'fabric of childhood' identifies that relationship between the social world we live in 'structure' and the individual's capacity as a meaning maker – their 'agency'. This interconnection is summed up in this definition of agency that notes the crossover between social structure and the active nature of the individual...

> *[Agency is the] Contextually mediated capacity of the individual to make meanings that inform actions, that are relationally situated and morally constituted and which are framed within a range of elements that make up children's personal lives.*
>
> (Frankel, 2017, p. 97)

Fig. 11 shows the relationship between our context, our personal lives (who we are) and the meaning that we make. This is significant in our ambitions to understand the learner. For what we are saying is that for us to be able to understand value, voice and vision, we need to be aware of these broader social dimensions that are influencing them. The diagram offers a simplified way of illustrating this process. We are *all*, children and adults, constantly filtering those social factors around us in relation to our personal lives and sense of identity.

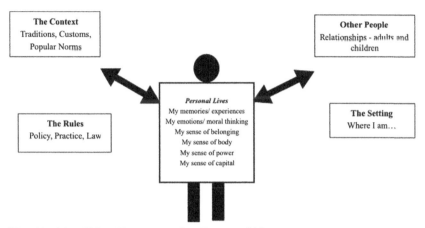

Fig. 11. Identifying Forces on Our Personal Lives.

How we come to interpret and make sense of the social world we are part of, through the way we see ourselves and come to be seen by others, impacts on our created sense of identity. In turn this directs how we come to act or re-act in our social world. Identifying these associations is crucial for developing our understanding of our learning connections and through them an assessment of our value, voice and vision.

LEARNING WITH AGENCY

Our agency is not a tap that can be turned off, it is always on; what changes is the nature of the opportunities within which we can exercise that agency.[21]

We are constantly assessing our value, voice and vision, *even when we don't have the freedom to practice* them. This realisation helps us to understand why discourses like the becoming, ominous and malleable learner are so damaging, but also how we can change the narrative, the story about ourselves, when we start to recognise the learner has agency

---

21 Explore the idea of thin and thick agency (Klocker, 2007). Agency is thinned by structural factors such as gender and ethnicity, limiting but not preventing the individual from their capacity to make meanings.

By acknowledging agency, we can establish a foundation that strengthens value, voice and vision.

Learning, in the following definitions, is active and dynamic in nature. What it means to be a learner can only be understood through a recognition of agency.

The two central definitions of learning that have always challenged and resonated:

> *Learning is the process of creating knowledge by making sense of your experiences.*
> *(Watkins, Wagner, & Whalley, 2000, p. 5)*

> *Only the individual child makes sense, understands and learns.*
> *(Pollard, 1994, p. 22)*

Both these definitions start by valuing the active, involved and meaningful capacity of the individual as a learner. They both make us question not only how we position learners in their learning, but what role the adult plays in enabling that learning. Learning is not something done to the child, but something the child does and can do. Learning is a process where the individual draws from their external experience, internalises these and makes new understandings – meaning making. Learning is a positive action carried out by a competent individual who is capable of making knowledge and meaning as a result of their experiences.

As we start to see the part played by the individual as a meaning maker, Chris Watkins and team (2007) invite us into the world of 'effective learning', with extended elements to learning such as:

- Active learning
- Collaborative learning
- Learner-driven learning/self-regulated learning
- Learning to learn

The learner has, thus, taken on a whole new set of characteristics and capabilities. Agency has brought life to the learning process, recognising that learning does not happen in a vacuum but is a part of our day-to-day lives – the people we are with and the places we are in and how we see ourselves (who we are). Being a learner is not a singular task, performed in certain places, at certain times; it is a multidimensional part of our functioning as humans, as we constantly respond to our experiences, drawing on these to create meanings.

Our approach aims to emphasise – we are always learning, we are innate learners! The next step is to connect the learner – to their learning!

Extending the Conversation

Research has highlighted the transition that takes place on entering school, as the child 'learns to be a pupil' (see Brooker, 2002). It draws our attention to the social processes of adaption as the individual finds ways to settle in and 'belong'. Imagine that process of adaption for different learning settings you are connected with – what is the learner encouraged to think and do, so that they 'settle in' and are accepted. How does imagining or re-imagining this process change depending on our views: whether we see the learner with agency or not?

4

WHAT IS LEARNING FOR?

Now, what I want is, Facts. Teach these boys and girls nothing but Facts. Facts alone are wanted in life. Plant nothing else, and root out everything else. You can only form the minds of reasoning animals upon Facts; nothing else will ever be of any service to them. This is the principle on which I bring up my own children, and this is the principle on which I bring up these children. Stick to Facts, sir! (Charles Dickens – Hard Times).

Competition is a vital force in inspiring innovation and challenging entrenched economic and political power but too much competition and comparison at an individual level can generate a permanent state of anxiety and make it harder for people to align their expectations with their actual capacities – perhaps the best route to personal happiness.

(Goodhart, 2020, p. 257)

How we think about the learner matters, as it deeply influences the purpose we attach to learning itself. In this chapter, we think about what is learning for. In the context of a constantly changing world, this chapter explains the need for a transition from an obsession with learning as performance, where targets and results related to cognitive regurgitation are all important towards a model of learning that is about a deeper relationship with knowledge and how we might use it as part of navigating our everyday lives. As, in the last chapter, we get the chance to add to our awareness of the barriers and enablers that impact our sense of value, voice and vision (Fig. 12).

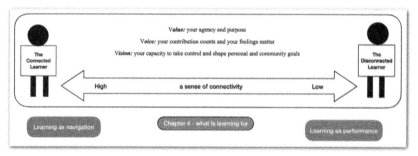

Fig. 12. Chapter 4 Overview.

A STANDARDISED SOCIETY

School, seems like a pretty good place to start this conversation. Although we are aware that our ambition in this book is to encourage thinking about learning beyond the classroom, school offers a common, understood focus to apply different theories on learning and how they impact on our identity as learners.

The drive for compulsory schooling was an outcome of the industrial revolution[1] (Scott & Gratton, 2020). As factories focused on a new level of production, the value of standardisation grew. Uniformity and predictability became central to a mode of production where one would

(1) take a source material,

(2) expose it to a defined and repeatable process,

(3) test – (discarding those products that did not reach the standard),

(4) release the product to the market for a recognised value (as defined by the quality of materials and the intricacies of the production process it was exposed to).

Business created a model of control and predictability that maximised profits and protected the lifestyles of the upper and middle classes. Compulsory schooling emerges and draws on this mechanistic model. The correlation between a 'source material' and a 'child' are unmistakable as the image of production above becomes an allegory for children, school and their ultimate place in society.

---

1 The industrial revolutions that have marked the last 200 years started in late eighteenth century, followed by a second in late nineteenth and early twentieth century and a third late 1990s.

Harry Hendrick's (1997) research on the history of childhood talks about the defining role compulsory schooling has played in the way we think about children. It marked a social process that centralised understandings of the child as well as set expectations for their role in society. Not only that, compulsory schooling was seen as a means to address social challenges that were caused by the increased presence of children in towns. As such it was school attendance and not learning that was important, as it brought children into defined and manageable spaces. This satisfied the machinery of society for control by (a) ordering a future workforce and (b) providing opportunities for children to be socialised into the role defined by society. Fast forward well over 100 years and those same themes of managing children as a 'project' or indeed a 'product', continue to apply. In a review of the school system by Berry Mayall, influential in the emerging field of childhood studies, she contributes to the underlying obsession with children as a 'source material' that adults must work on. Under a heading 'contextual factors influencing learning and behaviour' (Mayall, 1994, p. 125) draws out these themes:

(1) school is defined by a commitment to adult centric practices focused on shaping the child as a future being,

(2) school only works through a reliance on the demonstration of adult authority

(3) within school, adults see children as a project to be worked on

(4) That as a result of their experience within school – children see themselves as an object

In our efforts to examine and explore learning identities, an assessment of compulsory schooling where children see themselves as 'object' – without agency – and adults see children as 'project' has come to represent the status quo.

This view of 'education' has left a deep legacy. Schooling continues to encourage thinking of the child/learner as a source material – who exposed to a defined and repeatable process we call schooling, and tested according to various means of assessment – is then released into society with a recognised value – based on qualifications achieved.

These attitudes, influence societal perceptions of learning and the learner in terms of where learning happens, what learning includes, what learning is for and of course, who is allowed to learn.

LEARNING AS PERFORMANCE

Our English system (themes of which are reflected in many other countries) is defined in terms of academic performance that relies on extensive testing. I have on many occasions been told by teachers, as we are sitting talking about learning, how rare spontaneous opportunities for learning are. They speak of time and pressure to deliver what has been prescribed for them, ticking topics off 'the list', dreading the consequences of not completing these to the required level. Notably, this stress around performance targets is not just felt by the teachers but by the children and their families.

In his book 'Head, Hand, Heart', David Goodhart (2020) spends time assessing the current educational landscape. He highlights the focus on 'cognitive ability' in which success is defined by results. Those results carry associations of 'value', with very real consequences for learners in terms of how they perceive themselves and how they are perceived, as they create easy to see markers for 'acceptance'. Goodhart notes how we laud the 'brightest', whereas other qualities such as 'character, integrity, experience, common sense, courage and willingness to toil...command relatively less respect' (2020, p. 4). Where these other qualities are a focus for attention in one part of the system, there is no guarantee they will be acknowledged in another, for example, more progressive learning in primary school may be rejected at secondary school. In short, Goodhart summarises this obsession with performance in the following way,

> ...in recent decades in the interests of efficiency, fairness and progress, Western democracies have established systems of competition in which the most able succeed and too many of the rest feel like failures. (2020, p. 3)

It is that perception of failure that adds to a poor learning identity, creating a weight of anxiety as we continually struggle to find ways to align our actual achievement with ambitions, targets or expectations that are set. Practices that induce such doubt within the school system, hardly offer a strong foundation for lifelong learning (and UN SDG 4). For many, this assessment of 'cognitive ability' has been fused with Intelligence Quotient (IQ) or 'g' (general intelligence) as it is perceived as easy to measure. For example, as Goodhart notes, children at school in the United Kingdom may take CATests (Cognitive Ability Tests) and United States – SATests (Scholastic Aptitude Tests), which act as tools to separate out those with perceived greater 'cognitive ability' than others (see our earlier discussion around ages and stages). The place of these tests in education has and continues to be used to classify those that deserve the opportunities provided by being accepted to courses or to streams of learning that are focused on higher achievement. Such tests become a tool that defines investment and day-to-day practice, worse it defines limited learning experiences and learning identities. Goodhart asks, 'if g, as revealed by IQ type tests, is just a form of pattern recognition should it be afforded such a large space in educational and career selection processes' (2020, p. 57). We would suggest even more important, is the impact that such a focus has on the way that children (and adults) adopt a negative learning identity which affects their view of themselves as learners.

A system where the underlying purpose is to achieve exam success means that children's experiences are defined by their perceived ability to reach those cognitive goals, with ongoing implications for our learning identities as adults. And if you 'fail?' The following extract, from research with 10- and 11-year-old children in England, highlights children's thoughts on the compulsory SATests (Standard Assessment Tests)...

> *I think they're just for, like to see what group you go in, I think they are really important because you need to see whether you're clever or not. Cos if you went into the lower group and you know everything that they were doing, then you're not gonna have anything to dare you? You're not gonna learn anything new are you?*
>
> (James, 2013, p. 144)

The conversations and quotes that follow reflect a deep consciousness amongst the children that these 'tests' are critical to how they will be grouped or streamed in secondary school and as a result whether they are seen as 'clever' or not. This regular self-assessment was played out in wider classroom activities as children sought to balance success alongside feelings of disappointment and shame. It is the internalisation of 'being a failure' that such practices cause, that leads to a particularly concerning aspect of Allison James' review – the extent to which these assessments taken at 10- and 11-years old, just before a child enters secondary school, become a marker of future aspirations. As one child says 'Yeah you won't like get a job or something, you won't get a very good job will you if you don't take them [the SATS]' (2013, p. 146). What is being demonstrated here is not a system that is focused on strengthening learning connections but one that is only interested in limited and partial assessments of success and failure. For this child, by 11-years old, they were already *defined*.

The issues with using cognitive ability as a marker for driving practices in schools is passionately expressed by renowned academic John Hattie, in the following extract in relation to streaming…

> …what bothers me is the in-school class systems. I take tracking, streaming, and the effect-size supporting; these are very small indeed. But the equity issues are frightening. It's reinventing the class system within the school, separating those who have and those who have not. In many schools, you can walk the classrooms and count the colour – and the race discrimination via ability grouping is just not defensible. Nearly any one in the lower SES track is denied the challenging material, and when some students boost their investment and start to make progress they can often never catch up as they have been denied access to the more challenging material. This is indefensible in our society.
>
> *(Hattie & Larsen, 2020, p. 274)*

Hattie makes the connection between streaming and disadvantage, it is a similar point to one made by Malcolm Gladwell (2008) who links IQ to a seed which needs the right environment to grow. What's notable is that a favourable environment for this is strongly linked to a higher socio-economic status. Like Hattie, Gladwell argues that practices that focus on IQ only act to extend the gap between the haves and the have nots. IQ was never intended as a one-dimensional tool to fix, what has been called 'unchangeable intelligence' (Dweck, 2016), it was intended to do the opposite. In drawing on the work of Alfred Binet, the French educationalist who was an innovator of IQ, Carol Dweck (2016) explains that IQ testing was established to offer a marker to directly support and enable the learner to receive the right 'training, practice and above all method'. As a result, learners are enabled to 'increase our attention, our memory, our judgement and literally to become more intelligent that we were before' (2016, p. 10).

A rising pressure on the way we view IQ as a means for categorising the learner represents a challenge to standardised testing, demanding a greater focus on 'adaptive competence', which more strongly reflects culture and an individuals' background (Sternberg, 2014). It is on this basis we can explore what forms part of a broader assessment of intelligence recognising emotional and ethical reasoning as two additional dimensions. There is more of course that could be said here, but the point is that our obsession with performance shapes the way that people think about their learning identity. Indeed, as a response to the practices that are a consequence of a focus on performance, writer Alfie Kohn (2011) notes how the way we think about ourselves as learners is driven by a search for acceptance that sees us directly assessing our ability to achieve set targets and to follow the rules that our system creates. The result is that being able to 'reach the required levels' and 'follow the rules' become the core measures through which to measure ones learning identity (both in terms of the way learners see themselves but also the way they are seen by facilitators). As a result the learners' value is *conditional*, their voice is *insubstantial* and their part in contributing to a wider vision – *irrelevant*.

It is a way of thinking about learning that Chris Watkins (2008) talks of in terms of how policy approaches have led to a depoliticisation, a demoralisation and a depersonalisation in schools. Depoliticisation reflects the pressures on the teacher to conform to given criteria. Demoralisation flags the limitations schools face in fully being able to support the moral dimension of individual and community growth. Finally, and perhaps most worryingly, he emphasises that depersonalisation reflects a system that is simply not set up to value the individual as 'one size fits all' (2008, p. 7). Under these conditions, the range of identities available to pupils is severely limited such that children themselves are concerned about their value should they not fit the criteria that adults have established. As one 11-year old said in relation to taking standardised tests, 'So I'm frightened I'll do the SATS and I'll be a nothing' (Watkins, 2008, p. 7).

Ken Robinson writes, 'if you run an education system based on standardisation and conformity that suppress individuality, imagination and creativity, don't be surprised if that's what it does' (Robinson & Aronica, 2016, p. xvi). Retaining an image of learning that represents standardisation only reinforces out of date attitudes and practices that drive disconnection. Learning, that acknowledges the learner with agency, offers a very different focus, one of positive engagement.

LEARNING AS NAVIGATION

If we are to avoid a model of standardisation that limits space for the individual learner, then rather than learning being defined by reaching set targets, it needs to focus on *how* we reach those targets. The how will be different for every learner, and will alter during their learning journey. The importance of such a shift is based partly on a realisation of the agentic capacity of the learner, the learner with agency, but is also the more pragmatic response. Scott and Gratton make plain in their work the New Long Life, 'in the absence of change, this form of education system [learning as performance] will simply be preparing people for a life that no longer exists and for jobs that are no longer available' (2020, p. 165). The need to address what learning is for, becomes fundamental to our social system as a whole.

As commentators are highlighting, the 'change' will include a shift in the type and nature of jobs available and therefore what we do for 'work' and for how long (possibly increasing the time we have for hobbies[2]). Scott and Gratton, mentioned above, offer a valuable reflection on the nature of the changing world and the impacts this will have on society, including our relationship to the work place. They suggest one major change will be a move from the stability of a single job held for many years, to having different and more temporary jobs that require the need to demonstrate a range of competencies. No longer, they argue can education be about the need for 'students to acquire knowledge' (that knowledge is out there[3]), it needs to be about 'the notion of learners who acquire skills and the ability to apply them' (2020, p. 166). This encourages us to think about learning in the following way ... (Fig. 13).

	Learner
Space for learning	Across home, school and community
Time for learning	Lifelong
Required Output for learning	Acquire skills and ability to apply them

Fig. 13. Learning Across Time and Space.

As we have already explored, the current education system favours cognitive ability, which has created a hierarchy of roles within the work place. Significantly however, IQ, associated with the speed with which one is able to recognise patterns and make sense of them, reflects what Artificial Intelligence (AI) is increasingly capable of doing.[4] In the 2021 Reith Lectures, Stuart Russell talks about industrial change in relation to those traditionally 'good' or prestigious jobs being taken over by computers. So where do we fit in and what is learning for?

---

2 This can already be seen in relation to the move by some to a four day week (BBC News, 21/2/23). It raises interesting questions about our leisure time and how this might be used and the opportunities for 'learning' that it involves, although notably this idea of technology saving us time is not new (The Conversation, 1/10/2017).
3 Recognising the accessibility of the World Wide Web and the information it contains highlights that the challenges centre on managing and evaluating data.
4 Computers can data mine, AI can knowledge mine using algorithms but application to create knowledge will always be dependent on human interpretation – for more see Tsai (2013).

Goodhart, who we heard earlier, says 'computers are very good at analysing symbols, it's the messiness of the real world that they have trouble with' (2020, p. 237). It is by embracing our 'social' capacity that we start to emerge as distinct from computers. It is in our skill to engage with the messiness (indeed to learn from it) that we demonstrate our uniqueness. Goodhart offers the example of AI providing analysis of data to a medical practitioner, but it is the human doctor who will then discuss the diagnosis with the patient. Russell in his Reith Lectures offered another scenario relating to teaching children to learn in which he suggested AI would struggle as it would not recognise the multidimensional nature of what was going on – it could not grasp the social complexities – the messiness of learning!

Indeed, it is by embracing the messiness of learning that we can extend the importance of skill sets beyond recognition of cognitive ability. In his book the Happiness Curve, Jonathan Rauch (2018) reflects on those that have explored 'wisdom', with the significant finding that it is not cognitive ability, but rather a capacity to navigate and draw meaning from the messiness of social interaction that marks out the wise.

> *Again and again, modern scholarly definitions mention certain traits: compassion and prosocial attitudes that reflect concern for the common good; pragmatic knowledge of life; the use of one's pragmatic knowledge to resolve personal and social problems; an ability to come with ambiguity and uncertainty and to see multiple points of view; emotional stability and mastery of one's feelings; a capacity for reflection and for dispassionate self-understanding. You might think that people with the fastest mental processors would bring more cognitive power to bear on reflection and therefore would be wiser; but voluminous research finds that raw intelligence and wisdom simply do not map to one another, at least not reliably. In fact, on some dimensions, such as wise reasoning about intergroup conflicts, cognitive ability and wisdom, seem to be negatively related.*
>
> (Rauch, cited in Goodhart, 2020, p. 280)

Practically, by embracing what Scott and Gratton call those 'human skills' (experimentation, risk taking, experiential learning, collaboration, creative problem solving (2020, p. 167–168)), within the education system that learners will be prepared to complement AI and other technological developments. This they note, with reference to research that involved 10,000 top managers does not mean forgetting those efforts that have seen a major investment in STEM courses, but it does mean these need to be supported by displaying the 'very human skills' of 'being a good coach, empowering others, being interested in the well-being of the team, being a good communicator and listener and having a clear vision and strategy' (2020, p. 167). It brings us back to the need to focus on the social dimension of learning, which Stuart Russel refers to as a need for a concentration on the human world, rather than just the physical world (Russell, 2021a). A culmination of this, he envisages, may see engineering qualifications redefine themselves as 'managing and maintaining happiness' courses, with additional programmes on being 'life architects, curiosity enhancement agents, and resilience coaches' (ibid).

It demands we reprioritise our curricula. Goodhart, flags this in relation to the need to see a shift from courses whose raison d'être is cognitive ability, or what he terms 'head' to an investment in programmes of study that focus on 'hand' and 'heart', reflecting 'a missing conversation about educating people for democracy and for mental health and physical well-being' (2020, p. 277). In 2016, a report from the OECD (2016) marked the changing way in which people were recognising the world of work.[5] Notably, countries acknowledged the need for this shift through internal policies to promote lifelong learning and related skills. This has been responded to in each of the United Kingdom's devolved parliaments with aspirational documents that promote alternative ways to think about learning. Wales calls for 'ambitious, capable learners who are ready to learn throughout their lives' (OECD, 2020a). Northern Ireland is working towards a 'culture of lifelong learning' (OECD, 2020b), Scotland has created a skills model to promote a transition from school to work (Skills Development Scotland, 2018) and England has just published a White Paper 'Skills for Jobs: Lifelong Learning for Opportunity and Growth' (Department for Education, 2021). Frameworks on their own are not sufficient as they need to be supported by a change in mindset. For, not only is how we see the learner important but also how the learner thinks about themselves!

LEARNING IS FLOW NOT 'WORK'

In Creating Learning Cultures, Ron Ritchhart (2015) recognises the historical connection which saw the move from children in factories and then into schools. It brought with it a language around 'work' that has become ingrained in compulsory schooling. That spectre of 'work' is all around us in schools, referring to phrases such as, 'time on task', 'classroom management', being 'accountable for results', right through to students receiving 'rewards'

---

5 See www.oecd.org/education and look at the range of resources on twenty-first century Learning.

for performance to the naming of work books, work time, work periods and home work. Rictchhart shares a piece of research (Claxton et al., 2011) in which the researchers listened to classroom talk – discovering that 'work' was used 49 times more than 'learning'!

The result of this for the learner is that the focus within a classroom is around doing 'work' – 'how long does this have to be', 'will this be on the test', driving conversations that are related to the destination (or final goal), rather than the journey itself (the process of learning). Addressing this, Ritchhart suggests, allowing teachers to move from 'monitoring the work' to 'listening to learners', from 'are you finished' to 'what have you done so far', from 'what number are you on' to 'what questions are surfacing for you', from 'are you ready to move on' to 'what does that tell you' (2015, p. 45). This reflects a focus on process and the journey, rather than merely the destination. Mihaly Csikszentmihalyi (1997) concept of flow (mentioned in Chapter 2) sought to explore the conditions that allowed people to flourish, as he emphasised enjoyment and creativity, alongside a focus on happiness, well-being and positivity. Flow should be part of the way we think and talk about learning. Whereas, work requires us to focus on what we 'produce', flow allows us to focus on the journey that we take.

> *Csikszentmihalyi's recalled in an interview how he would watch painters in their studios and how he was fascinated by their ability to forget everything while working. He was also surprised by what happened when they were done: They'd finish a work of art, and instead of enjoying it…they would put it against the wall and start a new painting. They weren't really interested in the finished painting. What these artists were after, Csikszentmihalyi realised, wasn't the finished work itself but the experience of full immersion and absorption in the act of creation.*
> (Claremont Graduate University, 2023)

A change to language allows us to redress the restrictive elements of performance offering a very different statement on the purpose of learning. We will return to think about language in Chapter 8.

LEARNING TO LEARN

Ritchhart's writing makes broader points around culture; however, his discussion on learning and knowledge, deep or surface learning, growth and fixed mindset gives us vocabulary to expand our view of learning.

The focus on how to manage knowledge, rather than seek and retain it, is a key feature of a drive to broaden our expertise as 'navigators of learning'. We need to search for links between knowledge and awareness of appropriate skills and strategies that might support how that knowledge is turned into understandings and used.

> **Case Study**
>
> *I remember spending some time with a group of children who, for one reason or another, called themselves the Bumblebee Club. All the members of this 'club' were children who found it hard to be in the classroom. They struggled to recognise any value in themselves as learners. The first activity we undertook together, involved me asking them to draw themselves and list inside their self-portraits the skills they had as a learner. Outside their drawing they could write the skills they wanted to develop. Everyone drew the picture and then started to write. But, when we came together not one child had assigned themselves a 'skill' they thought they had, only skills to aim for.*
>
> One of the challenges that the Bumblebee Club faced was that 'learning' for them was defined by actions that reflected a destination related to performance...
> 'Complete the next 5 maths questions'
> 'Write a narrative of life as a viking'
> 'Read this and answer the questions that follow'
> Over the coming weeks, despite a growing awareness of their potential as learners, they still struggled. Their biggest challenge was a lack of confidence, how to navigate the tasks they were being asked to do. This uncertainty, drove disconnection from learning, as a result the children disengaged and finding other ways to pass the time often got into 'trouble'. The group needed an awareness of the processes of learning. The steps that are involved in learning becoming visible, enabling connection and bringing confidence in managing their learning activities.
>
> 'Learning' is not a frequent topic of conversations in schools. In our conversations with teachers and children on the process, the steps involved in learning are taken for granted rather than acknowledged. John Hattie (2009) calls for us to 'make learning visible' as do we! Our aim is to offer our contribution to a process of making learning visible

> and help you to create lifelong positive learning identities. As we saw in Chapter 3, Chris Watkins et al. (2007) identified four components of effective learning of which 'learning to learn' is the least engaged with. The reason for this they argue is a lack of a 'template' to make this part of their thinking and as a result teachers don't put it into practice. Until this happens, practices that reinforce 'learning as a performance' will continue.

As part of 'thinking about thinking' or 'learning about learning' we want to explore metacognition. Daniel Mujis and Christina Bokhove (2020) review metacognition and suggest,

> ...metacognition is 'instructions we give ourselves on how to do a particular activity or task.
>
> (Mujis & Bokhove, 2020, p. 7)

It offers a model for managing an experience and for 'processing' the data that one elicits from that experience – as we 'create knowledge'. Our intention is both to highlight its place and value and show how it contributes to our discussions on the agency of the learner. A template and related vocabulary allows learning to be seen as more than having to 'be quiet', 'listen' and 'follow the next instruction', but to be part of conversations on managing the process itself, as learners move from what David Perkins terms the 'tacit learner' to be a 'reflective learner' (1993).

It is that sense of having knowledge about ourselves, the strategies we might use and how those strategies might be employed that form part of the focus of the learning process.[6] Such knowledge enables learners to explore the different components needed to support a learning task, which feed into that broader sense of self we talked about in the last chapter. This visibility, paves the way for wider application as the learner recognises the aspects that apply on a Tuesday afternoon in maths or on a Thursday morning in PE. Situating the individual at the centre of their learning journey, they command their use of 'strategies' and reflections, enabling their ongoing exploration of a task. It is in

---

6 The metacognitive process reflects, as Muijs and Bokhove (2020) highlights – Declarative knowledge – what we know about ourselves; Procedural knowledge – knowledge about the strategies; Conditional knowledge – why and when to use those strategies.

the link between awareness, reflection and application that opportunities arise for making this metacognitive components visible. This is emphasised by one online resource (The Cambridge Assessment for International Education, 2023) that highlights the interrelated aspects of the learning process as they discuss planning, monitoring, evaluation and reflection. This is explained through questions such as:

Planning – 'what am I being asked to do' and 'what strategies will I use'

Monitoring – 'is the strategy working' and 'do I need to try something different'

Evaluation – 'How well did I do' and 'what didn't go well'

It is through thinking about these different aspects of the learning process that we begin to get a sense of learning as an 'art' (which consequently creates the fantastic image of the learner as an artist). In this process, Watkins et al. (2007) highlight the place of reflection. Indeed, in his definition of the self-regulated learner – it is this sense of reflection that stands out for Zimmerman (2002). He says of the self-regulated learner...

> ...these learners are proactive in their efforts to learn because they are aware of their strengths and limitations and because they are guided by personally set goals and task related strategies...these learners monitor their behaviour in terms of their goals and self-reflect on their increasing effectiveness. This enhances their self-satisfaction and motivation to continue to improve their methods of learning. (2002)

For Watkins et al. (2007) this is summed up through four key areas of attention:

- Noting about learning
- Conversations about learning
- Reflecting on learning
- Planning and experimenting with learning

As a response to this thinking and within the wider context of navigating change – we present four key 'stages' for reflecting on the processes involved in any learning journey.

The Learning Framework – Making Learning Explicit

(1) Have an Idea

(2) Talk and Listen

(3) Give it a Go

(4) Keep on Learning

Our steps are intended to make learning more explicit more visible, a need that a particular encounter with Jack directed . . .

> *Jack like members of the Bumblebee Club found it hard to recognise any positive learning attributes in himself. During our early conversations he did share that he was good at doing tricks on his BMX bike. So, I asked him if he could 'teach me'. We agreed we would need the bike in school, as well as a framework that might help Jack structure his 'lesson'. We discussed what this would involve and mocked up a format that might work. The bike came into school and Jack set about sharing with me how to do a 180 twist on his bike. We used our learning framework making notes (and video recording) as we went.*
>
> *I didn't quite manage the 180 that time, but I certainly understood how to do it! Jack shared clearly and effectively this journey of learning, captured under the headings of the framework. As Jack and I chatted, Jack saw that this learning could be transferred to the classroom. It wasn't long after that that Jack was sharing with his class the learning framework and explaining how this could be used by his classmates.*
>
> *It was a remarkable transformation. Jack had been able to make connections, seeing his potential, attaching his value as a learner to the task of learning itself. For the first time Jack was able to see himself with a positive learning identity.*

The learning framework:

(1) Have an Idea

(2) Talk and Listen

(3) Give it a Go

(4) Keep on Learning

appears ordered and structured the reality is 'messier'. Sequential steps become a process jumping back and forwards and repeating steps in between different parts of the process.

This wonderful description by Kline of a learning journey explains the rollercoaster ride...

> *From the frustrations, to the white flag, to the stripping down, to the trying, to the wondering, to the noticing, to the piecing together, to the being wrong, to the trying again, to the noticing again and the being wrong again, and the not turning away, to the impressive results (and changed lives and organisations), and to the ongoing intrigue of the never-completely-there seeing of what works, of facing what doesn't and of watching the pursuit find itself.*
>
> (Kline, 2020, p. 18)

Using the learning framework acts as a 'compass'. The learner can plot where they are, where they have come from and where they might be heading next. 'Learning as navigation' equips us to respond to the ups and downs of formal education, but also those informal challenges we might take on, offering confidence that we have the knowledge, skills and strategies to make our way through.

Extending the Conversation

John Hattie in conversations with Steen Larsen says that part of the point of visible learning techniques is to help those students who are not successful with current strategies they use in school to find new ones. Hattie goes on... 'That, by getting the teacher to shut up and the students to talk about what they're doing, you're more likely to hear the strategies they're using. You're more likely to understand how they're doing it' (2020, p. 36).

What is your response?

5

HOW WE CAN ALLOW LEARNING: IMPACT OF SELF AND 'OTHER' ON OUR LEARNING IDENTITIES

Interviewer: Is school a place where you belong?

Child: Yeah. But there can be things that can stop you, like bullies, and just really mean people. And sometimes you can get teachers that don't like you.

(Frankel, 2018, p. 160)

It seems that connecting with others is fundamental to a good life and having the means to cope with the challenges that life creates.

(Scott & Gratton, 2020, p. 77)

For too many adults the answer to the question 'how we can allow learning' is by control. It is teacher/facilitator/educator/instructor – directed. We suggest that 'control' cannot offer the means to develop value, voice and vision and so cannot strengthen positive learning identities and constrains the processes of learning.

In contrast, it is only with consent and meaningful mutual relationships that we 'allow' ourselves to recognise our place and purpose as connected learners with agency and so can maximise what might be gained from any learning experience.

We intend to examine the underlying ethos with which the learner is 'managed', and the impact on how we assess our value, voice and vision and position ourselves on the 'connection continuum' (Fig. 14).

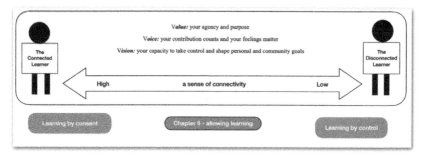

Fig. 14. Chapter 5 Overview.

We suggest two positions, one marked by an effort to enforce learning as a means of control and, secondly, a model of learning that is mutually beneficial, where both learner and facilitator have a shared purpose; we are naming this 'learning by consent'. Learning by consent requires a level of awareness of the individual and those social filters that influence their meaning making. It is through acknowledging the need to focus on meanings and emotions that we are given the chance to think more deeply about the individual and how they position themselves as learners. By explicitly noticing and referring to previous experiences, both good and bad, we identify and mitigate impact in order to learn for the next time around.

LEARNING BY CONTROL

Obedience defines day-to-day practice in school – from standing still when the whistle goes, to lining up, sitting quietly, putting up your hand, only eating at set times, using the bathroom with permission, following the set timetable in the same way each and every day! However, obedience is also about the way one responds to direction and the ability to complete the tasks that have been set. Such practices drive compliance, control and order and reinforce the place of school as a socialising force where children, given the correct instruction, will grow up to be rule-following adults, contributing to the work place and fulfiling their duty as citizens.

Rules

In a very telling account of his experiences in the education system in the United States, John Taylor Gatto (2005) profiles 'school' for him. It centred on obedience as a basic response to finding a way to just get through compulsory schooling. Resulting practice meant that the learner never got to think too deeply about anything other than showing an adherence to adult authority and following the chain of command. As Gatto says, 'the truth is that schools don't really teach anything except how to obey the rules' (2005, p. 21). The result is the 'dumbing down' of the individual learner as the teacher focuses on, what Gatto terms, 'seven key lessons' that each emphasise adult control, with the onus on the child to accept the rules and be obedient to the way adults 'do' school. The model that Gatto presents is not only relevant to the way we think about children at school, but also to our ambitions as lifelong learners. Below we have taken Gatto's seven lessons and re-worked these a little, showing how those dominant discourses from Chapter 3 impact practice. We highlight the link between the nature of the practice and the focus for learning that results, one that is clearly centred on control rather than empowerment (Fig. 15).

Control based practice in schools	Resulting Learning...
1. Know the facts not the meaning	
follow a prescribed curriculum that does not follow a logical order	Learning is about mastery of unrelated facts not about engaging with context or depth.
2. Know your place	
Students must be assigned to a particular 'class' and often to defined places in that class	Learning is about accepting the place (and information) given to you by those in authority (impacting ambitions and reinforcing disadvantages)
3. Stick (only) to the programme	
One must follow the timetable at all costs	Learning is not about spending time on what you are interested in but the ability to manage tasks you are required to do within set time lines (learning = work).
4. Tow the line	
Reward comes from following what you are told to do without question	Learning is about suppressing our individuality reducing the risk of being emotionally vulnerable.
5. Only proceed under guidance	
A good' learning is reflected in children waiting for a teacher to tell them what to do.	Learning is only 'good' if conducted within a defined scheme of learning, accredited by those with the requisite intellectual authority.
6. Achievement is marked by awards	
Teachers define what is recognised as a valued learning practice.	Our value as learners is dependent on external evaluation, as Gatto notes 'people need to be told what they are worth (2005: 10)'
7. Just get used to 'big brother'	
Children are to be watched over and scrutinised by adults at all times	Learning is about a process that requires you to be constantly monitored, reviewed and judged.

Fig. 15. Rule-Based Learning.

Learners will engage with the sentiments expressed in these headings in different ways, although their place in learners' experiences is pervasive. The fact that these principles underpin practice ensures that it is hard to escape the determination to 'control' the learner. This desire to 'control' has an impact on our sense of value, voice and vision as learners, disrupting learning connections. Below, we look in a little more detail at two examples.

Surveillance (Just Get Used to 'Big Brother')

The connection between being accepted as a learner and complying with those in authority is reflected in the part schools play in driving the citizenship narrative.[1] Traditionally the state has relied on the family to provide surveillance and be responsible for ensuring the obedience of its children as they move between school and their place, the wider community. However, this contract has eroded, with school increasingly being seen as the prime site through which the requirements of the state can be enforced. Experts in the area of school discipline and surveillance have noted 'a shift in punitive measures over the last decade' as schools respond to a 'culture of fear'. It has been argued that 'as schools have increasingly become expected to respond to a broad range of societal ills and concerns, including child protection, terrorism, drug abuse, obesity and violence, many have introduced evermore-invasive technologies and practices so as to be seen to be doing *something*' (cited from Deaken et al., 2018, p. 4).

It is that 'need' to do 'something' that is particularly problematic within a landscape that recognises the learner as ominous and is already set on control. The anti-terrorism 'Prevent' initiative in the United Kingdom has produced a number of examples of the impact of this surveillance. Prevent is one part of the UK governments counter terrorism strategy, designed to stop people from becoming radicalised into terrorism.[2] In practice, how Prevent comes to be applied has very real implications for the learner and how they might be enabled (or not) to learn.

> *A four year old boy was referred to Prevent after he said that he and his father had 'guns and bombs in his shed'. However, all this was linked to the computer game Fortnite. 'The child's mother believes that if her boy where white and not a Muslim he wouldn't have been considered at risk of radicalisation'* – Guardian – 31/1/2021

---

1 See Bacon and Frankel (2013) – discussion on the changing way in which the notion of citizenship has been assigned to children, in school and the wider community.
2 For more see https://www.theguardian.com/uk-news/prevent-strategy.

> *An eleven year old boy was referred to Prevent after saying he would like the school to burn down during a fire drill. Acknowledged by officers that this was just an individual who was struggling at school, it still lead to his parents having to fight for his name to be removed from related police databases. Guardian – 26/1/22*

> *Officials have denied claims a spelling error led to a 10-year-old Muslim boy, who wrote he lived in a "terrorist house", being spoken to by police. The family of the pupil, who attends a Lancashire primary school, claim he meant he lived in a "terraced house". Miqdaad Versi, assistant secretary-general of the Muslim Council of Britain, said he was aware of dozens of cases similar to that of the schoolboy.*

> *"There are huge concerns that individuals going about their daily life are being seen through the lens of security and are being seen as potential terrorists rather than students," he said. 'This is a natural consequence of the extension of the "Prevent Duty" to schools.'*
> BBC 20/1/2016

Such examples add to 'school' as a channel for authority. The result is that even though these practices may not directly impact all children, it does reinforce adult power, with implications for creating effective relationships in classrooms and how we think about ourselves as learners.

What is particularly troubling about this reliance on control is it is seen as a means to 'allow learning'. An example is 'zero tolerance' (the immediate suspension and exclusion of children from school) that emerged from the United States, with versions in the United Kingdom, Australia, Canada and other countries. The initiative grew out of a need to manage gun crime, where those themes of protection are clear. Its application has spread to include bullying, fighting, swearing, disruptive behaviour and wearing certain clothing (Welch & Payne, 2018, p. 215). In England alone the use of such policies sits alongside what appear to be increasing numbers of suspensions – the latest figures for Autumn 2021/22 are the highest for the first term on recent record[3] (Gov.UK 24/11/2022). These policies not only convey messages about school

---

3 There were 183,817 suspensions in the autumn term of 2021/22 compared to a secondary high of 178.412 prior to the pandemic and a figure of 129,151 in 2016/17. Note our review here is based solely on Autumn terms as this reflects the latest figures (gov.uk – 24/11/2022).

and authority but also they become a further marker of inequality and division, as disadvantaged children are disproportionately affected.[4] Such that

> Some teachers' and administrators' presumptions about minority students intellect and academic status may inadvertently influence the types of disciplinary response students receive for displaying behaviour that is different from that frequently exemplified by middle class white youth.
> (Welch & Payne, 2018, p. 222)

A Climate of Acceptance (Know Your Place)

A culture focused on control has implications for learners. In research I undertook with children in school, none of whom were likely to ever be excluded; there was a clear sense that the adults (at school) were 'authoritarian purveyors of order', who children were required to be obedient to. Their characterisation of adult authority is reflected in the following extract taken from a drama that a group of children put together. The 'teacher' is shown responding to an incident . . .

> Stop there! Go against the wall, you shouldn't bully in school.
> (Frankel, 2012, p. 162)

Questioned on their enactment of the teacher shouting at a child, the actor in the role of the teacher responds...

> Of course it's fair, you shouldn't have been talking or nothing, we're teachers.
> (Frankel, 2012, p. 163)

These characterisations reflected wider themes around the arbitrary way that teachers can behave as they reinforce their power

Mia: *The other day we had these cards that we had to make ourselves and some of them didn't work properly and he [the teacher] just chucked them in the bin, but we spent time on making them*

SF: *How did it make you feel?*

---

4 This disparity is reflected in economic status ('whether you receive free or reduced price lunches is another strong predictor of harsh school discipline') as well as gender and disability. Notably research shows the impact of such practices do not just affect the individual but the learning community as a whole.

Louis: *Upset*

Mia: *Annoyed*

Andy: *Because we've spent ages on them*

Mia: *We've spent our time and you think what's the point of doing it if you're just going to chuck it in the bin; there is just no point. And he would shout at you if you didn't bring it in but then he just chucked it in the bin*

SF: *So how did you deal with it, do you just accept it or what?*

Andy: *You have to accept it because if we shout at them [the headteacher] she will probably suspend us*

For this group of children, the requirement for obedience is absolute, not to be questioned. For children's relationships this created a sense of the 'unfair', which was expressed in a range of emotions from annoyance, frustration and not feeling appreciated. It was only by acquiescing to adult authority that the children demonstrated a way to maintain a constructive association with their teacher as they ensured (i) they were seen by the teacher to do what they were told and (ii) they accepted adult instruction (repressing their feelings that this engendered).

As we look across, both these sections an experience related by my own children seems somewhat apt.

> *As I was writing this section one of my children announced over breakfast that "her friends school had turned into a prison. If she hadn't got rid of her nail varnish then she would have got a detention or possibly suspended. They went round checking everyone's finger nails and uniform. And if they are late to lessons they get suspended". The same day she came home from her own school to say how she had been told by a lunch supervisor that the nail varnish she had on two fingers was against school rules. No opportunity for negotiation or discussion, the nail varnish was visible so the crime had been committed, resulted in plenty of tears and this encounter being the one that defined 'todays' experience of school.*

> *A couple of weeks later (as I am still working on this section!) my daughter reports how her friends school was planning a protest. Teachers found out about this and through locking doors and issuing threats manage to avert this student action. However, it seems that this desire for pupils to 'engage' is not isolated but a growing national phenomenon. At a time when their teachers are*

> taking strike action, it seems an ongoing sign of the system that to maintain control, schools are hiding behind arguments around safeguarding, rather than presenting participative practices that demonstrate a desire for effective engagement that recognises a commitment to a shared goal for their learning community.

Children's perception of adult power is very real. John Macbeath (1999) illustrates a 'spiral of trouble' as imagined by a 13-year-old learner, which shows the progression from 'fooling around' to 'being suspended'. It emphasises how a lack of time for conversation and finding out leads to a reliance on teacher authority in driving actions. Notably greater mutual respect is identified as the antidote.

Assessing one's identity as a learner based on obedience (Kohn, 2011) means that for an individual to align themselves with being a 'learner', they are required to suppress their own feelings of what is fair and just, and acknowledge the authority of the adult – who is always 'right'. These perceptions of power should not be underestimated in terms of the impact they have on the way children (or any of us) identify as a learner, shutting down learning conversations and increasing the anxiety of the learner to act in ways approved by a formal instructor. As a result, learning identities become conditional, with very significant implications for our sense of value, voice and vision and our learning connectivity.

LEARNING BY CONSENT

Being Known and Understood

'Learning by consent' builds on the premise that the relationship between the 'teacher' and the learner, is one of partnership and trust, with a shared ambition for a common goal. A desire to control learning, to micro manage every aspect is exhausting, unfulfilling and contrary to creating a sense of value, voice and vision that will endure lifelong. We want to encourage a foundation for a relationship that grows partnerships and trust and a shared ambition for a common goal. Learning by consent demands we recognise the different elements that shape our individual connectivity and how those interact to inform the way we create meaning. As such, 'consent' must have a more explicit place in learning.[5]

In some early research I did (see Frankel, 2012), children shared their relationships and the way these made them feel; this was key to whether an experience

---

[5] Mountford (2020) explores some of the wider issues around consent and its place in shaping children's everyday experiences.

was labelled as a 'learning opportunity'. For example, if the child acted in a way that was not seen as acceptable, if there was a willingness from the adult to have a conversation and to discuss this, it was marked as a learning opportunity (the child's value, voice and vision was recognised). This stood in contrast to a child being shouted out for the same act. Encounters where the child felt *known* and *understood* maximised the potential through which children then 'created knowledge by making sense of their experiences'. As such, to enable learning, it requires that we, both learner and facilitator, are in touch with how we and others are feeling, as this will impact on our interactions in a positive or negative way effecting how we come to position ourselves on the 'connection continuum'.

How You Feel and How You Learn

When we talk about emotions here, we are focusing on the meaning we attach to our feelings as we reflect on the world around us and how we react to 'socially and personally constructed' ways of *being* shaped by our ambitions and goals (Smith, 2017, pp. 13-14). The focus on emotions has been noted (from different disciplinary starting points) as of significant value in furthering our understanding of children's engagement with learning (see Frankel & Mountford, 2021). It is that inquiry that has formed a major part of the conversations that we have had with children in schools over the years.[6]

What such conversations showed was our emotional response to those around us, how we were feeling, influenced how we learnt. As part of this, we asked just over 800 children some simple questions about how happy they felt in key spaces (the classroom, playground and home), whether they felt they fitted in, and how that space enabled their learning. The results – *being 'happy' and 'fitting in' not only informed children's attitude towards the importance of learning but also their ambition as learners*. This was reflected in a number of ways (Fig. 16).

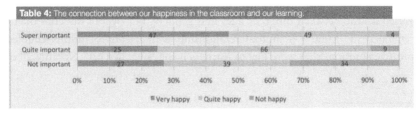

Fig. 16. Happiness and Learning.

---

6 For a more detailed account see EquippingKids (2017, 2018).

First, the happier you feel the more likely you are to value your learning. We can see this here with learning in the classroom; children who described themselves as happy were more likely to see learning as 'super important', in contrast to those who were not so happy and saw learning as 'not important'.

Second, how you feel in a given space correlates to how it is rated as a learning setting.
Positive feelings were also linked to how you came to value the experiences within a particular space. For example, being 'happy' in the classroom meant you were more likely to embrace the value of the classroom as a space for learning.
This was reinforced by the finding that 'home', which was the space most children felt happiest and fitted in best, was the space children marked out as the best place to learn, just ahead of the classroom.[7]

Home offered an emotionally safe place, where that sense of being known and understood was easier for the children to recognise (both in terms of perceptions of oneself but also in respect of relationships with adults). Home also had wider benefits that supported positive emotions, which came from making choices and doing activities that were 'fun' (*you can learn stuff on the trampoline*). Here the aim is not to make an argument for all learning in schools to take place on a trampoline (although that would be interesting), it is about recognising those connections between emotions and the learning experience they engender that is important, allowing us to think about maximising opportunities in different spaces and through different activities (home, school and the community).

In discussing what supported the feelings of happiness at school, similar to home, the children talked about the value of 'fun' and having 'choices'. They also talked in detail about friendships, their relationships with adults and the nature of the learning activities themselves. How these impacted learners varied a little between different ages and genders, but overall the core theme remained the same – a mutual relationship with friends or adults enabled positive emotions that were key to learners being 'switched on'. Notably all of

---

7 The findings from this research (EquippingKids, 2017, 2018) even in communities where headteachers recognised challenges at home, many children still saw home as a space in which they were happier and felt more able to learn. This raises some very interesting questions around both belonging and home as a space to learn (For more on home see – Frankel & McNamee, 2020).

this links to a positive sense of value, voice and vision as key to experiencing effective learning experiences.

Filtering Our Feelings

However, to fully understand the nature of an interaction on our sense of value, voice and vision, it is important to look a little deeper. We have already started to see above that mutual relationships and belonging are central to an individual's emotional connection to their learning, the following three themes enable us to take this further as we focus even more on those factors that inform our sense of self and ultimately our learning identities. These three themes are...

i. our power and the power of others,

ii. our body – being similar or different,

iii. our social capital – and the pursuit of status within our communities.

Power (Our Power and the Power of Others)

Perceptions of power impact on our sense of self and as a result of our learning identities.

Power is such a defining feature in relationships between adults and children (teacher and learner) that it seems a good place to start. Power is too often viewed in one dimension, reflecting a hierarchy where some individuals and groups sit above others (the powerful teacher and the powerless pupil). However, power is a much more subtle force that forms a constant feature of our day-to-day interactions. Stephen Lukes (2005), although not writing in relation to children, highlights the centrality of power in influencing social life. He notes the constant tension on the individual as they continually make assessments on power, based on where they are and who they are with. These assessments influence our sense of value, voice and vision and where we position ourselves on the 'connection continuum'. It is a search for a balancing of power in relationships that becomes important, as we weigh up both how we see ourselves and how we see others (Fig. 17).

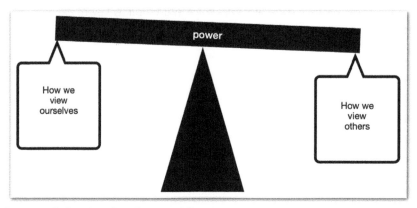

Fig. 17. Balancing Our Sense of Power.

The implications of this function of agency in relation to learning is set out in Table in Fig. 18.[8]

	How we see ourselves (us)	How we see others (those around us)
impacting learning	*The mutual self*	*The mutual other*
	The learner has a sense that they are known and understood, and are confident in their sense of belonging. Learner is open to engagement and ready to participate.	Accepted as a guide or collaborator, contributing directly to the individuals learning experience. Recognised as acting for and in the best interests of the learner.
	The powerless self	*The powerless other*
	Learner lacks confidence. Hesitant. Searching for ways to hide or disguise weaknesses. Has higher tolerance for accepting interventions from those seen as more powerful.	A target to be continually judged and assessed. Has to prove their credentials to be allowed to 'join in'.
	The powerful self	*The powerful other*
	Learner's sense of power over others - can be over bearing or dominant, not listening to the ideas of others. Learner's sense of power in themselves - can be empowering - encouraging the learner to set new boundaries and targets for personal bests or raising expectations for those around them	Regarded in terms of the threat they pose. Learning opportunities framed in terms of direction, surveillance and control - all backed up by the fear of sanction or admonition. Age in itself can inform a sense of greater power, a factor adults need to be aware of and mitigate.

Note, this is a simplified overview, that offers some idea for how perceptions of power might inform a learning experience.

Fig. 18. Perspectives of Power.

---

8 For more on these categories for exploring power see Frankel (2012).

An insight into power, however, cannot be seen in isolation. For if we want to achieve that sense of equilibrium, understanding the worth associated with mutual relationships, it also demands that we examine two further features of identity, (1) the body and belonging and (2) social capital.

Body (Our Body – Being Similar or Different)

To make sense of belonging, we need to start by thinking about the 'body'. A focus on the body enables a reflection on how we come to position ourselves in relation to others. Essentially, it can be summarised as a measure of similarity and difference, although in practice it is more complicated than that. Anthropologists have argued that social order is defined by how we distinguish ourselves from others. As the eminent Mary Douglas says, 'it is only by exaggerating the difference between within and without, above and below, male and female, with and against, that a semblance of order is created' (1966, p. 4). Within this, our sense of self, as recognised in our own perceptions of our body, becomes 'a canvas upon which identification can play' (James & James, 2004, p. 19). We evaluate those around us in relation to 'actual body' (body shape, age, sex), the 'styled body' (clothes, jewellery, gender) and 'performance' (what you can do with your body). We then make decisions about who we wish to be aligned with and those with whom we wish to belong.[9]

This is highlighted in the extract below, in which these two 11-year-old boys show the sophisticated way in which they explore who might be a 'friend'. Shared interest, ability to perform in a game, an exploration of whether there is a shared ambition to engage, giving them a compliment, are just some of the tactics discussed in framing a sense of similarity and identifying the 'mutual other'.

Tim: *Somebody who doesn't talk about rubbish, like someone who like talks about the same things that you like, say if they like football and you like football*

Matt: *You have got the same interests*

SF: *How would you know that*

Tim: *You like try and make friends*

Matt: *You sort of like give them a compliment and then start off a conversation*

---

9 For a more detailed exploration of identity formation in children see James (1993).

Tim: *You might just ask them a few questions like what hobbies do you have, what interests*

Matt: *Also if they were playing a game you could join in and then you sort of find out*

Tim: *Like if I saw someone wearing a Chelsea shirt I'd talk to them about football, Chelsea*

Understanding this process has a range of implications for learning. We need to be aware of the social gameplay that takes place as individuals come together, with implications for the way we reflect on friendship groups and peer relationships. Acknowledging this also enables us to be more aware of the emotional reactions that might result from individuals learning together and the implications this has on their learning journey. Who we learn with – shapes our learning experience.

There is an additional theme in relation to body that it is also important to raise; perceptions of power are of particular relevance in a world where young learners are inundated with 'noise' about body type and appearance. The body thus becomes a focus for 'fashion' and 'trend' for what is 'sexual' or 'sporty', all of which can have implications for learning identities. Making the body a focus of discussion enables a greater focus on the destructive and negative way in which some have chosen to use the 'body' to demean, de-value and degrade others (and themselves). However, it also allows for a more positive narrative that challenges destructive thinking and offers a stronger foundation for empowerment. This drive to inspire this deeper understanding has in some ways been reflected in curriculum efforts linked to 'relationships', however this is only a starting point!

Social Capital: The Pursuit of Status Within Our Communities

Capital must be seen through its relationship with experience. We all have a library of experiences in our minds. How we come to manage those experiences and give meaning to them has been termed habitus, an idea developed by the French sociologist Pierre Bourdieu. Bourdieu's (1990) concept of habitus has been drawn on by theorists from childhood studies, connecting habitus (and this process of sorting experiences) to the notion of capital. Paul Connolly (1998[10]) makes this connection through research that highlights the context specific nature of identity formation, shaped by that search for capital.

---

10 Also see Connolly (2004, 2006).

Capital here is to be seen in relation to the value that the individual attaches to a particular action or set of behaviours – (a mix between how we come to position ourselves in relation to a social hierarchy and ambition). This assessment, as with those above, emanates from the individual, as they seek to process their sense of self in relation to both the space and those around them. Context is central to the perception of status. For example, what might be seen as of value to a group of children who run the eco club, in contrast to those in the football club, may be very different. Capital for the football team may be linked to speed or coping with competition, whereas for the eco club capital may be linked to research skills, environmental knowledge and an ability to communicate. Learners are not fixed to one group but will oscillate between different groups, applying different understandings and meanings in relation to actions and behaviours dependent on that changing relational and structural context that they find themselves in.

In the extract below, Mike (Frankel, 2018b, p. 159) talks about a time when his friendship with a group of older children was threatened, when he felt he could not understand what they were discussing.

SF: *So how does it make you feel when you're a bit confused*
Mike: *Quite funny to be honest*
SF: *So it's okay is it – you don't mind*
Mike: *It makes me want to make a joke*
SF: *So why would you want to make a joke*
Mike: *I'm not really sure, it's a natural reaction*
SF: *So when you're feeling not sure about your place in the group, you might try and make a joke*
Mike: *Yes or try and be funny*

Here, Mike finds his sense of belonging is challenged, and so he needs to act in a way to head off any chance he might be seen as being 'other'. He, therefore, recaptures the initiative by making a joke and bonding himself back into the group. This adoption of certain behaviours as part of seeking to achieve status with a particular group is a part of everyday life, including school. We only need to look at the vast array of Disney films to see the different 'cliques' associated with schools, and the clear characteristics and behaviour that are associated with different members of those groups (being sporty, musical, into technology and so on) and the status assigned to them. Many of these films then make a narrative out of the efforts for a character to achieve belonging by re-inventing who they are. The relevance of such themes in schools is very real.[11]

Re-imagining Discipline

As we reflect on 'allowing' learning in the context of 'learning by consent', it is important just to return once more to the theme of obedience, and particularly to discipline, as it is such a defining feature of the school experience, and such a significant factor in shaping a sense of value, voice and vision. The discussions above encourage a more nuanced understanding around emotions and 'behaviour' in school. 'Discipline', rather than framing a one dimensional interaction that is adult directed (guilt assigned and punishment delivered), offers an opportunity for a learning encounter that acknowledges social impact and the need for restoration. Reflecting on restorative justice approaches in schools (see Hopkins, 2004), we can then explore more creative disciplinary policies and practices focusing on 'learning and relationships', where behaviour is explored in the wider context of the impact it has on learning. It respects learner identities, the identity of those who might have been impacted, and the wider communities' vision for learning. It raises important questions about what we mean by 'justice', a topic that is of real practical relevance in a learning community

To achieve 'justice', driven by a focus on 'learning by consent', schools and other learning settings, must meaningfully invest in steps that move 'discipline' away from an adult-centric act that reinforces power (which we have noted above is problematic in the context of an effective learning experience) to one that invites a greater shared responsibility for behaviour (within the context of preserving a connected learning environment). As with restorative justice, as noted above, a process emerges which enables learning opportunities in ways that seek to maintain constructive relationships and offer pathways for restoration. This all begins by enabling conversations to happen on how we feel and why.

Two conversations (Frankel, 2012) that always stick in my mind were with two boys in their final year of primary school. I was asking them about what happens when they do something wrong at 'school'. One of the challenges that Josh and Nat shared (two enthusiastic boys who often found themselves facing

---

11 Research reflects similar findings, for example, Andrew Pollard's (1994) seminal research on children's identities in primary schools and how children positioned themselves in relation to three groups the goodies, the jokers, the gangs, and how this impacted their learning experiences.

the ire of the adults around them) was that being 'told off' offered no real learning opportunity principally because, as Josh shared, 'well they never exactly explain because they haven't got a lot of time' (p. 165). The result is that the adult is unable to ascertain any sense of a working relationship (the scales are out of balance see Fig. 17) with the child and the resulting interaction is one that simply illustrates the adult power over the child. Josh and Nat also shared another example when they talked about their head teacher. Nat explained that in her case she is *quite good at sorting out problems*. The reason for this as Josh shared was that *she just sat us down and said 'what's the problem?' She listened to both sides of the story*. That willingness to make a connection to allow the boys to share their feelings and then to work together to explore a response created an encounter that both boys valued and as a result learnt something from – 'she gave us both a fair hearing'. This headteacher offered space, to learn by consent.

A learner can so easily be disconnected by the simple roll of a disapproving eye or a raised voice and left to feel they had failed (had fallen below that measure of acceptance based on obedience).

However, these two small examples highlight the meaning that comes from adults establishing mutual relationships, driving a process of 'learning by consent', where the perception is that the scales (of power) are balanced and the learner feels known and understood. It is in offering the time, within a context of trust that Nat and Josh were able to share their feelings and find a way of repairing and resetting relationships, an experience that contributed to building their learning identities...

- value – mutual respect
- voice – your voice counts too
- vision – you are part of the solution not the problem

It is an investment in value, voice and vision that should enable our approach to learning. Recognising that it is through creating space within which learners are able to connect with their feelings and emotions that we can look to re-position ourselves on the 'connection continuum'. Learning identities are not built through approaches that rely on control but on consent. The coming chapters explore how we might put some of this thinking into practice.

Extending the Conversation

Find out more about 'character education' and the way in which a deeper reflection on character can inform and shape our experiences of learning and as learners.

The Jubilee Centre (2017) share four pillars for enabling 'practical wisdom' that allows individuals and society to flourish. They talk about intellectual, moral, civic and performance virtues. Lucas and Spencer (2020) talk about 'performance character' – resilience, positive attitude, self-control, 'grit' and craftsmanship (p. 55). How we come to both define and measure character is still an area in need of additional research and investigation.

What value do you place on this area of inquiry and to what extent does character add to the way in which we are able to think about the 'connected learner'?

For Discussion: Nils Christie (1977) is one of a number who have written about reclassifying the way we refer to 'crime'. In a series of arguments Christie suggests that crime needs to be classified more in terms of the act being seen as 'conflict', 'trouble', 'problems' and/or 'harm'. It moves us away from the one-dimensional focus on the perpetrator and invites a deeper consideration of the emotions and feelings of those who were harmed, as well as those that caused the harm. As such we are encouraged to centre in on the 'harm' to the community that the act has caused. How and in what ways has this relevance in the context of your learning setting?

THE CONNECTED LEARNER IN PRACTICE

INTRODUCING THE CONNECTED LEARNER IN PRACTICE

Chapters 3–5 allowed us to explain the 'connected learner' in theory, through a focus on the 'learner with agency', 'learning as navigation' and 'learning by consent'. It gave us a chance to map a landscape which is littered with obstacles that might limit or restrict our learning connectivity, as well as recognising those ways in which connections can be enhanced.

The following chapters draw on our experience of learning with children, and offers a framework through which the ideas set out at the start can be put into practice. Although the second half of this book is written to enable school-based conversations, the framework has much wider application (for example, in a youth work context or adult learning centres) and in keeping with the arguments throughout this book, is applicable to all learners whatever their age.

INVITING YOU TO 'PLUG IN'

Developing a Culture of Advocacy

We identified five steps focused on maximising the connectivity within a learning environment, which in different ways link to value, voice and vision. The process is not linear, each step, is not an end in itself, but sets in motion conversations to trigger a re-imagining of your practice. There isn't a check list but we will explore some principles that can shape your discussions and form a basis for you to take positive action.

Chapter 6. 'P' – **p**ower up your learner centred ethos

Chapter 7. 'L' – nurture a '**l**earn to be' culture

Chapter 8. 'U' – **u**nify your language

Chapter 9. 'G' – **g**row meaningful opportunities

Chapter 10. 'IN' – **In**spire lead learner

> *About 15 years ago I walked into a school led by a friend and colleague John Fowler. Straight away the school felt 'different'. It was not the welcome by the staff at the front desk, it was not the displays on the wall, or the colourful fish tank in the corridor, it was not the neatly piled boxes to one side in the hall, it was the children. There was purpose in their walk and a confidence in their greeting. It was as if I had entered, the fabled offices of a big Californian tech giant (at least in my imagination), and despite there being no table tennis tables and no-one on scooters (again my imagination), there was a sense of passion and purpose in the movement of the 'young executives' that were around me. You sensed a hunger to pursue the next task and an excitement about what might be discovered. In short there was an overwhelming desire to learn.*
>
> (Frankel & Fowler, 2016)

It is that dimension of practice that we want to be the focus in Part 2. Each of the chapters has been written to use as a resource to support professional conversations.

To frame these conversations and to support an environment designed to enable all learners to 'plug in' and connect, our approach encourages you to search for a 'culture of advocacy' – defined by 'establishing the voice of the child' and 'amplifying the voice of the child' (Frankel, 2018a). This model that invites adults, in any space that they share with children or other learners, to ask themselves a series of questions to reflect on their practice. This approach supports strongly our ambition to advance practices that lead towards connected learning.

Each of the Chapters 6–10 follows the format

(1) Have an Idea
We give you our idea(s) – as a question that offers a starting point for a learning journey of your own.

(2) Talk Listen and Plan
We share some information with you. You can use it to trigger your thinking, either independently or with others – build conversations!

(3) Give It a Go
Provides a practical way in which you can explore the question that we set out – this forms a basis to expand on and gain further understanding and we hope develop your own approaches.

(4) Keep on Learning
We will connect this thinking to the wider goal of the lifelong learner and share some final thoughts reflections and references that you might find useful.

6

'P' – POWER UP YOUR THINKING

The way we think about the learner matters. It shapes our methods, practices and ultimately children's experiences. So, if we want to create an effective learning environment that strengthens value, voice and vision, the starting place must be 'us'. Our job title or years of experience do not provide a 'pass' that allows us to 'skip' this step – if we are involved in nurturing learning experiences then it is important that we are continuously reviewing how we think about the learner.

1. HAVE AN IDEA

Question: Value, voice and vision is enhanced by recognising the *learner with agency* – how do you view learners?

2. TALK, LISTEN AND PLAN

Tackle Our Assumptions (the Value of a Detox)

> *Tackling our assumptions can be hard. I remember one head teacher who found it particularly challenging. He felt a weight of responsibility (based on his position and years of experience) that he should know how adult actions would impact on children's learning experiences. However, as we started to explore value, voice and vision he realised that what we were asking "were like no other questions" he, as the strategic lead, "was asked to consider". Simply*

asking children 'what does it mean to be a learner?' was highlighting the limitations of relying on adult assumptions.

One of the consuming challenges we have in today's society is the issues that arise when assumptions about individuals and groups have been left unchecked or unquestioned. In the context of our focus here on children as learners – potentially the most limiting factor in creating an environment in which children can connect are the attitudes of adults.

The way we as individuals come to understand children and think of them as learners does, of course, stem from many sources. These sources reflect our own childhoods, how we were parented and how we were taught. It may reflect our professional journeys, the courses we have done and our practical experience of working with children in schools. All this takes place within a particular cultural context, where society's thinking about children, presented by the media, politicians, celebrities and more, will influence us personally, within our peer groups and the institutions within which we work.

These will include

- Cultural traditions – religious beliefs of customs or conventions
- Formal policy – such as case law or government legislation
- Education/professional training
- Online trends
- Broadcast media/books
- Conversations outside the school gate

Each of these sources acts as a conduit for certain understandings of the child, some may be progressive (the learner with agency), however much will continue to amplify *noise* about what children 'lack' (the learner as becoming, ominous and malleable), informing and shaping the assumptions or stereotypes that direct our own meaning making and limit the opportunities we create to further value, voice and vision with wider application beyond the child learner.

Note How Our Assumptions Shape Practice

Eminent anthropologist Mary Douglas (1966) talks of the basic need we have as humans to categorise and sort as part of ordering our social lives (see Chapter 5). Through labelling others, attaching meanings to particular groups, we can create short cuts – or stereotypes, that help us to quickly make meanings within the plethora of day to day interactions that we are part of. As Nigel Rapport, concludes these stereotypes, which draw on those assumptions we have discussed (becoming, ominous and malleable), present 'a shorthand: a source of consistent, expectable broad and immediate ways of knowing the social world' (1995, p. 280). The recognition that this is part of simplifying the way we process the social world, reducing the deeper thinking we need to do, highlights why it is important that we are prepared to question the assumptions that we hold. For if these assumptions inform our sense making, if they contribute to the short cuts we rely on to categorise people and consequently the actions we choose to take as a response, then they are incredibly significant. If those assumptions are based on misplaced understandings, then the source for our decisions and the choices we make in relation to other people, in this case learners, could simply be wrong.

The reason why the way we think about the 'child' and the 'child as a learner' matter so much, is because it influences our practices and through this shapes their experiences; with implications for their learning identities. Paul Connolly observed teachers working in an inner city school and looked at how race and gender came to shape children's experiences. Teachers saw black boys through a particular lens, applying a stereotype that assumed meanings that reflected the 'learner as ominous'. The result was that the actions of black boys were dealt with, by staff, with a much harsher recourse to disciplinary practices than their peers. It created a cycle in which the boys came to internalise those assumptions as part of their identity as learners. As Connolly reflects...

> *What I want to suggest...is that teacher pupil and pupil-pupil relations form a complex feed-back cycle where the actions of each tend to influence and exacerbate the other. In this sense it could be argued that the over-disciplining of Black boys tends to construct an image of them, among their peers, as being 'bad' and quintessentially masculine. This in turn, provides the context where Black boys are more likely to be verbally and physically attacked. As a consequence, Black boys are more likely to be drawn into fights and to develop 'hardened' identities, which then means they are more likely to be noticed by teachers and disciplined for being aggressive. The cycle is thus complete.*
>
> *(Connolly, 1998, p. 114)*

What Connolly's work shows, is that it was an 'understanding of the child' based on assumptions that reflected wider societal attitudes of the 'learner as ominous', linked with race and gender, that shaped practices that consequently impacted children's learning experiences. It has been and continues to be assumptions about children that affect so much of children's sense of identity as learners.

It is in our willingness to assume, that the toxicity of our own thinking sits. In spite of adult intentions to act in the 'best interests of the child', without engaging with children's voice, these adult centric perspectives, remain that – adult centric and, are often full of misunderstanding and misrepresentation of the issues. The repetitive nature of such thinking and how that informs practice and experience is illustrated below with reference to themes from Chapter 3 (Fig. 19).

Image of the Learner	Adult Assumption	Adult Centric Practice	Child - Experience
Ominous	Learning through displaying control	Reliance on rule based structures and interactions	Constant supervision (acceptance is conditional on following rules)
Becoming	Learning directed by future value	To deliver curriculum aimed at future productivity	Always aspiring to achieve required grades (fear of failure)
Malleable	Learning aimed at moulding the passive learner	To define all learning experiences	Limits children voice and motivation

Fig. 19. Impact of Assumptions.

Power Up Our Thinking

John Fowler, a former head teacher and friend, mentioned in an early collection of thoughts relating to this approach... (Fig. 20).

> We all make assumptions and I must admit that schools and those of us involved in them are particularly prone to this. It is right that we challenge our use of those assumptions and the way they come to shape the perceptions we have of the children, and as a result affecting the way they come to see us. Fortunately, I have a constant reminder hanging in my home. It is one of those pictures that a child has drawn you that you know from first seeing it that you are never going to be able to throw it away. The picture is a

Fig. 20. Drawing of Mr Fowler.

> *portrait of me done by a 6 year old from a school early in my career as a head. There I am, moustache, tall, tie but with the biggest nostrils you have ever seen (and my nose is not THAT big). An artistic mistake? No of course not, for that was exactly how the child saw me! As he was seated in the front row of the assembly hall, there I was standing in front of him, and as he looked up what he saw was my nose!*
>
> *A few years later I read an article called Maverick Heads (Hay Group, 2002), it highlighted that need for schools to continually question assumptions. It challenged headteachers to push boundaries and 'cross the line', taking on those areas of misunderstanding that had limited children's place in the learning environment for too long.*
>
> (Frankel & Fowler, 2016, pp. 22–23)

This extract reminds us that assumptions are both ways. We will hold assumptions about children, and they will hold assumptions about us. Thinking about the learner and the implications for practice and ultimately learner's experiences, we can 'push those boundaries' as we 'power up our thinking'.

It is in the intentionality of our efforts to examine our assumptions that it allows us to establish a personal ethos that enables value, voice and vision as we take the position to look beyond assumptions and to engage with each individual as a connected learner.

A process to aid this reflection is set out below.

3. GIVE IT A GO

The Assumption Tracker

So having

- Tackled our assumptions (the value of a detox)
- Recognised how stereotypes shape our practice

How do we power up our thinking?

Well we refresh, review or revisit the image of the learner that we hold. It is that easy! But, this only works if we have a wider sense of the forces that influence and shape assumptions about the child or learner in the first place. Visualising the different parts of the jigsaw that shape how we come to see learners can be helpful. It shows the connection between attitudes, practices and experiences, which can be essential to challenge existing practice and promote change. It allows us to be purposeful and intentional in assessing the nature of the themes that influence how we think, and as a result how we come to act.

Have a go... (Fig. 21)

(1) Think of a specific learning space where you interact with learners

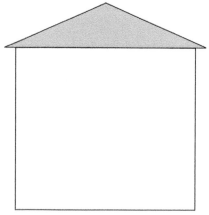

Fig. 21. Assumption Tracker 1.

(2) What 'noise' are you surrounded by?
What do you hear about THAT learning group? For example, what are the narratives about THESE children/learners? (Figs. 22 and 23)

- in the news,
- on social media,
- in the books you read,
- the courses you take,
- the traditions or customs you are part of.

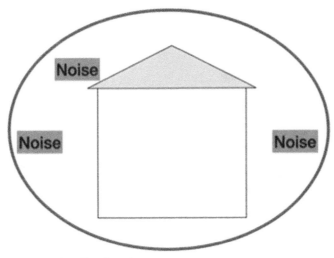

Fig. 22. Assumption Tracker 2.

(3) From that wider noise -
   - what noise is loudest in or around the setting you have picked?

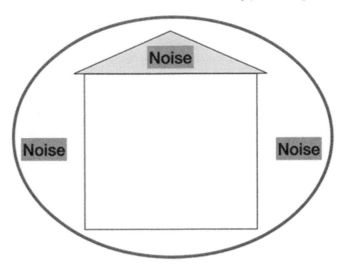

Fig. 23. Assumption Tracker 3.

(4) What image of the learner (child) do you have?
When you think about the learner what assumptions do you draw on, to shape your image (your way of thinking) about individuals or members of that group? (Figs. 24–26)

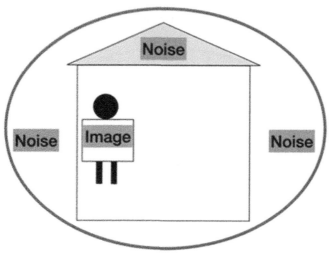

Fig. 24. Assumption Tracker 4.

(5) How does the way you think about the learner/child shape how you act – the practices you use?

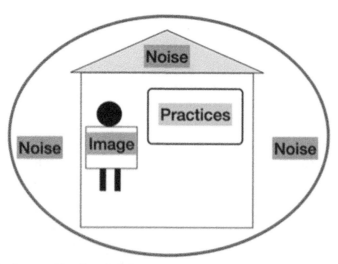

Fig. 25. Assumption Tracker 5.

(6) What are the learner's/children's experiences as a result of your practices?

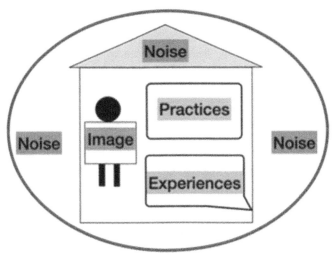

Fig. 26. Assumption Tracker 6.

(7) Are you happy with the practices that are in place and the experiences learners have?

How might a shift in your assumptions, enable a new image, new practices and new experiences? (Fig. 27)

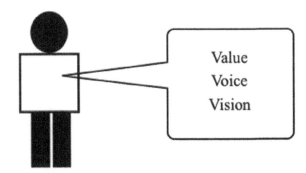

Fig. 27. Assumption Tracker 7.

4. KEEP ON LEARNING...

> **Extending the Conversation**
>
> As we think of the lifelong learners, we can see how different assumptions play out in different ways, informing interactions. *Age* can be considered alongside additional filters such as *gender, ethnicity and ability*, all of which contribute to the assumptions that we hold and which shape the way we think about the learner.
>
> This thought provoking video from the US non-profit AARP (American Association of Retired Persons) invites young adults to share their thoughts on older people before meeting them and undertaking a shared learning task together.
>
> The vividness of the assumptions that the young adults held and how these come to be challenged by the older people makes for very touching encounters. It reminds us of the need to be continually challenged to power up our own thinking, as we examine the assumptions we hold, and ensure our attitudes do not cause disconnection but instead empower each learner to build their value, voice and vision.
>
> Consider assumptions that have limited how you view the learner.

7

'L' – NURTURE A 'LEARN TO BE' CULTURE

This chapter is about exploring the culture for learning – whether that be in a school, home or community setting such as a dance or music class. The ability for a learner to 'connect' will be shaped by the culture within that space and the way it responds to those key questions of Chapters 3–5

(1) Who is a learner?

(2) What is learning for?

(3) How can we allow learning?

If we are to ensure effective learning connections it is important that we examine the 'culture' within our learning spaces in respect of these questions and how that influences a learner's value, voice and vision.

Such an examination must be continuous and evolving as we 'learn' and 're-learn' from one another. As part of this one action stands out in promoting effective learning identities and that is 'starting conversations'.

Being part of conversations is not only good for helping manage the day to day practicalities of learning, but such conversations also allow individual learners to feel consulted and involved at a deeper level, reinforcing their sense of value, voice and vision.

We all know the difference between conversations where we might go through the motions, hiding or protecting what we really feel, compared to those conversations where we open up and some of our inner selves is on display. In business, approaches to managing change demand the need to 'engage with people's inner theatre and underlying motivation' 2019: 84. It is the same for change within a learning community too, just as with business this adds a deeper and more nuanced understanding to the intra-personal, interpersonal, group and organisational behaviour. Leadership guru, Manfred

Kets de Vries, is clear that – 'to get the best out of people, courageous exploration and conversation need to be part of organisational culture' (2019, pp. 84 and 85). It is with this sense of 'courageous exploration' ringing in our ears that we should start to think more about our own learning communities.

1. HAVE AN IDEA

Question: Value, voice and vision thrives on partnership – *enabling learning by consent* – so, how would you define the culture of your learning community?

2. TALK, LISTEN AND PLAN

Don't Assume You Have Got It Right

One way of separating out cultures that might associate more with the connected learner at one end of the continuum and the disconnected leaner at the other is to reflect on a learning space in terms of it engendering a culture that emphasises the need for a learner to be 'taught to become' in contrast to a one where they might 'learn to be' (Fig. 28).

	Taught to become		Learn to be
Success criteria	Learning as Performance		Learning as Navigation
Children (seen as)	Disconnected Learner (Ominous, becoming, malleable)	vs	Connected Learner (Agentic)
Culture	Adult centric - learning by control		Co-constructed/ child centred - learning by consent

Fig. 28. Taught to Become vs Learn to Be.

Many of the trends relating to the *disconnected learner* are ingrained in society structures, we read about this in earlier chapters. The following research from 1971 shows the way in which institutional practice – ways of doing things, can limit good intentions and our own 'powered up' thinking. It highlights why our 'intentions' towards children are not always enough, even better would be a change of the 'culture' within a learning space.

> *This school felt it was very progressive in terms of children's voice and participation. To mark this, each class set out to create a*

classroom constitution as a way of creating a sense of community at the beginning of the new school year. The teachers felt very proud of this as an activity and felt they were directly creating space for children to be involved. However, what the researchers found, in conversations with the children, was that the wider culture in the school (one that was more focused around learners being 'taught to become'), meant that this activity remained adult centric and lacked the meaning to the child, which the adults assumed, it would offer. The researchers highlighted a number of aspects of the culture that limited effective participation (notably all of which are valuable cues for challenging practice today)...

(1) the teacher knows best

(2) children cannot participate constructively in the development of a classroom constitution

(3) children want and expect the teacher to determine the rules of the game

(4) children are not interested in the constitution

(5) children should be governed by what a teacher thinks is right and wrong, but a teacher should not be governed by what children think is right or wrong.

(6) the ethics of adults are obviously different from and superior to the ethics of children

(7) children should not be given responsibility for something they cannot handle or for which they are not accountable

(8) [An expectation that] if constitutional issues were handled differently [more responsibility given to children], chaos might result.

(Sarason, 1996, p. 217)

Based on their responses to the research we could assume that these teachers, at an individual level, had a progressive view towards the learner, however in the context of the classroom, and the culture of the school, their actions were shaped by a wider organisational culture that reflected ingrained assumptions about the need for children to be 'taught to become'. When, for the last 5,000 years, we reflect that 'organised' learning is synonymous with being taught (Watkins, 2005, p. 48), it highlights the size of the challenge. So, it is important that we do not assume or underestimate the barriers to overcoming institutionalised practices and the way in which these have interfered with that innate human capacity to learn. How do we review this? Start conversations!

Let Participation Be Your Motivation

As we seek to further conversations, it is important that we are clear about the 'motivation' that drives organisational practice towards children as learners (Frankel, 2018a). Traditionally motivations towards children have been dominated by an adult desire to provide for the child and protect them and to ensure they have a future place in society. In the context of learning this is translated into the duty to…

Provide: children have core basic needs met and are filled with the knowledge required to be an effective future citizen

Protect: schools act as supervisory force on behalf of the state to ensure children's safety and the wider harmony of society

We add in profit, to reflect the themes we discussed earlier and the relationship between education and the workplace.

Profit: (1) schools present '*their*' curriculum to define their place in the market (present a USP that ensures 'customers'); (2) schools collectively act to re-stock the next phase of the educational or labour pipeline (schools shaped by university expectations) and satisfy work place vacancies/requirements; (3) the image of the happy child can become an advertising tool to generate business (in both non-profit and commercial sectors)

The P's above reflect motivations that can be attached to what we see as the purpose for learning, perpetuating a focus on the child being 'taught to become'. However, there is another 'P'. That 'P' is participation.

Participation: enabling children's engagement in meaningful conversations that frame and shape their learning communities

By understanding participation and reflecting on it as the primary motivation for organisational practice, it enables a more knowledge based response to children's needs and their safety. It moves us from a model where protection and provision dominate, to a model where participation enables a focus on each of the other 'p's in an equal way, driven by the value of a child centred approach.

Creating a Culture Is a Community Task

We would argue that only in learning communities is the value, voice and vision of learners respected, connecting them to social as well as knowledge worlds with positive learning identities formed as a result. Chapter 5 profiled the relevance for the connected learner of 'learning by consent'. In practical terms this requires schools to look at what underpins their community, allowing a partnership approach to shaping and re-shaping school culture, recognising its evolving nature between different cohorts over time. As Chris Watkins notes, this does not necessarily mean having set principles in mind but it 'depends on the values which develop, and the best is achieved through a caring, pro-social, learning orientated approach to the relations between all parties' (Watkins, 2005, p. 50). Ethos, and the culture it enables, becomes a community project, that is far more than a fixed vision or mission statement, but an ongoing relational exercise that will evolve over time. This is brought to life in the example below, where Chris Watkins advances his compelling vision for a learning community.

> **Case Study – In Search of a Learning Community**
>
> Chris Watkins's research on school communities stresses the value in the journey. He talks about different levels of community, with the separating factor being the level of learner participation. These levels are...
>
> (1) Classroom as communities
>
> (2) Classrooms as communities of learning
>
> (3) Classrooms as learning communities
>
> Watkins reflects on how a sense of **classroom as communities** creates:
>
> - students that are more engaged
> - increased sense of belonging, leading to greater participation and motivation
> - shared responsibility
> - difference is not a problem and diversity is embraced
>
> This is all positive, however it should not be seen as the end point. For a greater shift we should move towards **classrooms as communities of**
>
> (*Continued*)

learning that enables the learner, to contribute, and their contribution is seen as integral in defining the space itself, bringing

- increased engagement in leading and high level engagement in the discipline
- learning from and helping each other
- motivation: to learn for its own sake, to make choices and feel responsible for what happens to them
- enhanced individual outcomes on important aspects of individual learning

However, what is so powerful about Watkins's work is that he is not prepared to accept this as a final destination either. He recognises the potential that an embedding participation offers, one that is centred on themes of mutuality and partnership, which were discussed previously. These learning spaces, **classrooms as learning communities**, are not about one party's ambitions to further learning, it is a search for a joint vision for learning that comes to take precedent.

...a learning community operates on the understanding that the growth of knowledge involves individual and social processes. It aims to enhance individual learning that is both a contribution to their own learning and the groups learning, and does this through supporting individual contributions to a communal effort. (2005, p. 57)

The result of such a community he suggests are the following…

- disciplined discourse becomes part of the community
- responsibility for and control of knowledge becomes shared.
- conceptions of learning are richer and co-constructive
- shared metacognition develops about the process of learning

We would add that these outcomes 'create positive learning identities', which can be further enriched over time. We extend an invitation to 'learn to be a community' and be continuously reflective about the culture within our learning settings. Through a process of meaningful engagement, that prioritises participation as a motivation, we can build a shared sense of community. It gives us a point to schools and learning contexts, which centres on the ambition to collectively frame a culture for learning focused on allowing *all* to recognise their identity as connected learners.

3. GIVE IT A GO

A. Rhetoric vs Reality

A. Have a look at the 'assumption tracker' from Chapter 6. You can take yourself out of the steps and insert your learning setting – it will allow you to assess the organisational thinking that centres on learners in that space.

B. By asking ourselves what is the motivation within a learning community, we can start to reflect on what underpins the ethos of our community. It is a process that invites opportunities to ensure there is a match between the rhetoric and reality! Using that to spark conversations can help to address whether our ambitions or indeed perceptions of a space match the reality of learners everyday experiences!

Explore some areas of practice and ask yourselves – where can you close the gap between the rhetoric and reality? (Fig. 29)

Area of focus	Ideas - shared as possible actions	Assessment - culture?	Assessment - motivation?	Steps to further your community...
		Does this reflect a 'taught to become' or 'learn to be' culture? Why?	What is the 'motivation' for this action? Why?	Conversation starters and next steps...
Website	(What ways can you ensure children's voices are more obvious on your website?)			
Parent mail	(What contribution do children make to mail outs?)			
Class room practice	(How can children take a more active role in shaping the curriculum?)			
After school clubs (be specific)	(How much choice do children in have in creating the programme?)			
Playground supervision	(What is needed to re-vitalise play time?)			
PE Lessons	(How can you improve engagement for all learners?)			
Outdoor learning				

Fig. 29. Rhetoric vs Reality Activity.

B. Review Your Learning Spaces

Using at least one of your own learning contexts and applying Watkins's categories, analyse and rate what is happening:

Classroom as communities

- students that are more engaged?
- increased sense of belonging, leading to greater participation and motivation?
- shared responsibility?
- difference is not a problem and diversity is embraced?

Classrooms as communities of learning

- increased engagement in leading and high level engagement in the discipline?
- learning from and helping each other?
- motivation: to learn for its own sake, to make choices and feel responsible for what happens to them?
- enhanced individual outcomes on important aspects of individual learning?

Classrooms as learning communities

- disciplined discourse becomes part of the community?
- responsibility for and control of knowledge becomes shared?
- conceptions of learning are richer and co-constructive?
- shared metacognition develops about the process of learning?

Additional Questions:

- Is value, voice and vision of learners respected?
- Are you connecting them to social as well as knowledge worlds?
- Are positive learning identities forming as a result?
- What is your final assessemnt of your learning culture having reviewed the questions above?

4. KEEP ON LEARNING...

> **Extending the Conversation ...**
>
> Creating a 'learn to be' culture is not just the responsibility of schools, but needs to form part of broader efforts across learning settings, from craft workshops, to corporate training days to being modelled in CPD (continuing professional development) sessions. A 'learn to be culture' is essential to enable learners and teachers to connect as part of building an environment where we can 'learn by consent'.
>
> How would you assess the learning culture in settings you have experienced? What was it that influenced those cultures and as a result positively or negatively impacted on your learning experiences?

8

'U' – UNIFY YOUR LANGUAGE

Every school has a language of its own – from the language of the children to the administrative language of the office, the playground, the classroom, the staff room, the senior leadership team, the governors and, of course, the parents – a range of stakeholders, all of whom might have a different way of describing and talking about the learner and learning. 'Unifying your language' establishes a shared understanding that breaks down barriers and enables a common basis for engaging with value, voice and vision and positive learning identities. By developing a unified language, we can all participate in conversations that help us to navigate our learning journeys through strengthening our learning connections.

1. HAVE AN IDEA

Question: Value, voice and vision are part of understanding how to *navigate our learning* – how do we create a shared language to support this?

2. TALK, LISTEN AND PLAN

The Power of Words

Our use of language and the meaning we ascribe to different words can be defined in how we position ourselves in relation to certain activities, such as learning. George Lakoff and Mark Johnson (1980) talk about metaphors and how they influence our everyday realities by shaping the way we come to give meaning to our actions.[1] There are a number of metaphors that are relevant to the way we think about learning. One striking example, that we looked at in Chapter 4, is the metaphor that 'learning is work'. "It is time to go and do our work", "here is your homework", "we must be quiet while we do our work". The association with work automatically invites an evaluation of whether the work is 'good or bad', conducted 'efficiently or not' and, of course, whether it has been 'successfully completed'. Part of our goal here is to challenge the language of a 'taught to become' culture and its obvious links to disconnection and instead explore how language associated with a 'learn to be' culture might enable more effective personal learning connections, increasing the ease through which the learner can connect and navigate their learning.

A Language for Learning

Establishing such a language, all stems from starting the right conversations. It is a process that offers an explicit way of bringing to life a proposed ethos around participation and partnership as a school moves to or seeks to maintain a 'learn to be' culture. Practically it not only offers a way to start raising awareness of ambitions to enable a greater focus on participation, but it also provides an important opportunity to consider the nature of language used to support learning, recognising that unless we share a common language for learning it is very easy to become disconnected.

In the last chapter, we have discussed culture and the value of getting the community involved in creating it. The table below offers an overview for how this might be developed, as the community becomes part of defining the values and the learning attributes that form part of that learning space. The table and related images present the conclusion of a series of conversations in one school who were reviewing their language for learning and shows how their (a) ethos, (b) values and (c) learning attributes all came together, setting a foundation to enhance their 'learn to be' culture (Figs. 30 and 31).

---

1 They provide, as an example, the following metaphor – 'argument is war'... 'your claims are *indefensible*, I've never *won* an argument with him, he *shot down* all of my arguments, he *attacked ever weak point* in my argument' [original italics] (1980, p. 4). The result, they suggest, is that such language becomes more than talk; it actually influences the nature of the practices we employ. How we negotiate arguments is shaped by this metaphor around battle. What would the difference be in a culture 'where an argument is viewed as a dance'?

'U' – Unify Your Language

School ethos	School Values	Learning Attributes
Vision for learning culture	4 or 5 key value based learning ambitions for each learner - connected to vision	Directly drawing on each of the values, define a series of attributes that makes 'learning' visible.
Our express yourself school: inspiring us to achieve and learn with confidence	Be Responsible Encourage Others Show Respect Try our Best	See below

Fig. 30. Ethos and Value in Practice.

Be Responsible	We *embrace new experiences* and learning opportunities
	We *explore different perceptions* and are prepared to think differently
	We are *able to recognise and share what motivates us* and those around us.
	We find ways to *direct and shape our own learning*
	We know how to *collaborate effectively* - good team work
	We recognise what it means to be a *leader*
	We are *nature loving* - caring for the world around us
Encourage Others	We are aware of *what we do well and what we would like to do better*
	We *set, monitor and evaluate our targets* and goals (encouraging others)
	We *recognise when our goals have been achieved and* help each other to *celebrate*
Show Respect	We *encourage creativity*
	We *value everyone's voice*
	We *express our feelings* and recognise the feelings of others
	We are able to *have fun* and ensure others have fun too!
	We are *effective communicators* who can share ideas
Try our best	I have a *good sense of my own identity* and am proud of who I am
	I know *when to take risks* and who to turn to for support
	I am *a reflective learner* who recognises the *value of making mistakes*
	I am resilient and courageous - I *have a go* and I *keep on going*

Fig. 31. Language for Learning in Practice.

To support engagement – each value is illustrated with an image (Fig. 32).

Fig. 32. Language for Learning in Pictures.

In practice the process of composing this language for learning can take time. It invites deep and important conversations around what the 'values' of the school are and what they mean and how they relate to defined 'attributes for learning'. This makes a conversation about values explicit, recognising that this conviction to establish moral purpose is a defining part of teaching (Pollard, 2014), but one that too often is repressed through unwritten rules and individual interpretation. The result of this is that schools can end up with a plethora of value-based language,[2] as different people or groups use a range of words to describe particular behaviours. By 'unifying the language', having those conversations that allow for a common (accessible and relevant) vocabulary brings clarity to what it means to be a learner.

Don't forget about the wider learning community: In the context of a school community, one group of stakeholders that is important not to forget in the drive to develop a language for learning are parents and carers.[3]

Using Clean Language

As we have noted, one of the challenges of reflecting on language in schools is the way in which certain words and phrases (like learning and the learner) carry particular meanings. Clean language an approach developed by David Grove, a psychotherapist from New Zealand, but which now has broader global application (Cairns-Lee et al., 2022), offers a means to 'elicit another

---

2 In a review of value-based learning, Arthur (2010) recorded a school with over 20 value based words.
3 One finding from the experience of learning during the pandemic highlighted – 'both now and looking forward, school leaders emphasised the importance of evaluating impacts and identifying the ongoing needs of pupils and failed for recovery, for example through staff, pupil and parent feedback and surveys' – (DfE, 2022, p. 31).

person's meaning in a way that is authentic to their experience' (4). At its most basic level, it is a series of 12 questions 'cleaned' of assumptions and metaphors leaving a blank space for the other person, whatever their age, to gradually clarify their understanding of what they really mean and want to say.

As a starting point, one might introduce these 'developing questions' into conversation

– and what kind of (…)?
– and is there anything else about (…)?
– and where/whereabouts is (…)?

(see McCracken, 2016)

Question: It looked like you were really into that task – what were you doing?

Answer: Oh we were learning

Question: What kind of learning

Answer: Learning together

Question: Oh, what can you tell me about learning together…

These developing questions can be added to with 'sequence questions' that allow a learning experience to be broken into a series of activities or remembrances – 'and then what happens…'. Finally, there are 'intention questions' that focus on the desired outcome and what is needed for these to be achieved – 'what would you like to have happen…'.

Through following principles that require the facilitator to

- Listen attentively.

- Keep your opinions and advice to yourself

- Ask clean language questions to extend your understanding of the other person's points

- Listen to the answers and then ask more clean language questions about what the other person has said (see Business Balls, 2023)

a greater understanding of an individual's perception of an experience will emerge.

The technique can deepen by exploring the metaphors used in a person's answers. This can bring new understandings of what is limiting someone and open up new possibilities for them in their thinking. The benefits of this approach to clean language (Walker, 2014), which are directly relevant to the wider ambitions being shared here, is that it...

- develops understanding of the individual
- addresses assumptions
- appreciates what others bring
- uses all the resources of the group (intelligence and experience)
- creates attention across the group

It is through establishing greater individual understanding alongside that broader group engagement that enables this focus on language to have transformative effects. A focus on language brings communities together – it unifies!

Build a Technical Vocabulary (Applying Clean Language)

When you use Clean Language in the classroom be prepared for a leap in learning. Colleagues have been surprised by the speed of impact. Children learn to think deeply and to express their ideas with clarity. They come to appreciate each other's specialness and to value differences. They learn to think about thinking and become more comfortable exploring challenging ideas... especially their own!
–Julie McCracken, primary school teacher in Sullivan and Rees, 2008, p. xiii.

Ensuring that language is not a point of disconnection for the learner is a key part of the efforts to create a shared language for learning. This can be built on by developing certain 'technical' vocabularies to advance and support engagement in relation to other elements of the learning journey that are a focus for that community, which at the least will ensure a consistency of understanding amongst lead learners. Ritchhart (2015), whose work we mentioned above, suggests a range of areas where a technical vocabulary may be of value, they include...

- Thinking
- Community
- Identity
- Initiative

- Mindfulness
- Praise and feedback
- Listening

Language to support how we learn is looked at in the Chapter 11, but here I want to highlight, in brief, four areas that are relevant to supporting value, voice and vision, which are...

- Emotions
- Participation
- Research or inquiry
- Non-verbal language

All reflect terms that are frequently used but which can be understood in a number of different ways. Here, we are only able to touch on these themes, as a way of illustrating how unpacking language provides opportunities that can form part of deepening learning experiences.

Emotions

Chapter 5 explored the place of emotions and feelings in how we might reflect on our value, voice and vision. Ensuring a vocabulary that allows the learner to engage with a discussion around learning, and those broader themes of well-being,[4] is undeniably a necessity in enabling a learner to connect. We will return to some practical tools that might be of use to support the development of this vocabulary in Chapter 11, however, here we just wanted to make the simple point that a language that distinguishes between 'happy' and 'sad' is not enough. Drawing on an illustration I have used elsewhere (Frankel, 2018a) that highlights an account shared by former head teacher John Fowler, we can see how rich a language around emotions can be and how this needs to be tuned in to the learners that one is enabling (Fig. 33).

> *In responding to low attendance at school by aboriginal children in Australia, it was noticed that children didn't feel that they were able to discuss how they felt. This then created a barrier to their learning*

---

4 New Economic Foundation's (2008) 'Five ways to Wellbeing' – (i) Connect – ensure strong relationships, (ii) Be Active – get moving around, (iii) Take Notice – promote curiosity, (iv) Learn – keep on learning and (v) Give – get involved.

and to their ability to effectively explore a positive learning identity. The language in schools for talking about feelings was simply not the language these children used.

For these children their emotional vocabulary was deeply rooted in their relationship with the natural environment - where they used different weather types to express how they felt. Making this part of the language they were able to connect to their learning allowed them to find a place in school. Some of this emotional vocabulary is shared below.

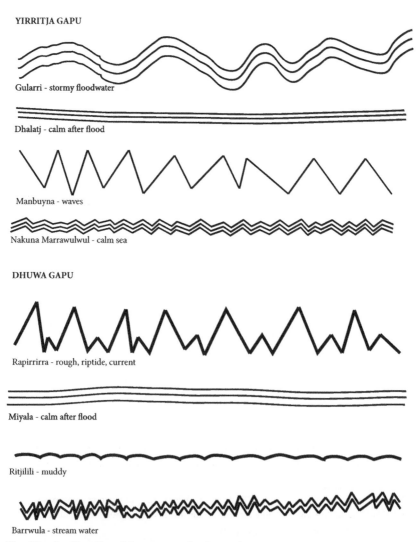

Fig. 33. An Emotional Language for Learning.

As this case study so clearly highlights, having a language to express how one felt was essential for these children to be able to connect and navigate their learning. Being able to start conversations that allow children to explore their feelings and know how to express these in constructive ways is key to building a resilient learning identity, as well as contributing to the level of understanding within the learning space itself.

Participation

We have already mentioned participation, indeed it is an area of significant depth that we are not in a position to explore in full here. The purpose of highlighting it is that it is one of those areas where it is very easy for an understanding of what 'participation' is to be assumed.[5] This then has implications, for example, for how we think about 'voice' in practice.

An outcome of giving time to explore the vocabulary we attach to participation is that it

(1) Allows us to break down the acts of participation

(2) Offers a basis for more meaningful engagement.

There are different academic models for participation,[6] which have in common a means for us to explore the divide between an act that might be 'tokenistic' and one that really holds 'meaning' for those involved. These models form a basis to assess the inclusive and relational basis that inform an encounter. Getting this right takes us towards terms like co-participation with an emphasis on the collaborative ways in which opportunities are framed.

In this brief reflection – it is a desire to see a shift from the learner as an 'object' where participation is not valued to one in which they are seen as a 'co-participant', established by a language of participation. It allows us to acknowledge thinking on 'rights' but also to extend this, as we consider practical ways in which the learner can play an active part in shaping their communities.

---

5 Tisdall Gadda and Butler, (2014) highlight how other languages outside of English have more expansive phrases and vocabulary for expressing participation.

6 For example Hart, 1992; Shier, 2001; Lundy, 2018.

Research and Inquiry

A language around research supports a community to ask questions and to answer them! Whether as a focus for teachers or support staff, a language around research can enable action-based research or a review of performance, however, it can also open up possibilities for learners to take an active role as 'investigators'.

Over the last few years, 'co-production' has emerged as an approach that offers a real focus on collaboration. It allows for a number of stakeholders within a community to be part of the process of identifying the areas for investigation and in exploring solutions. It is a format that, based on what we have shared elsewhere, enables children to take an active and meaningful role in shaping conversations within a learning community.

Research teams in schools allow children to not only shape the focus for an investigation, but also to take control of the data that result from their questioning. A simple structure might involve (see Frankel, 2018a, p. 109)

- (Have an Idea) Decide the nature and type of their questions
- (Talk, Listen and Plan) How they are going to ask the questions
- (Give it a Go) Capture and integrate the data
- (Keep on Learning) How will they present their analysis

It, therefore, arms children as the knowledge keepers, who then have an important part in sharing their findings and pursuing action. In schools this offers a meaningful addition or alternative to school councils. It is an approach that offers possibilities for children to be more involved in issues of significance within their community, both in terms of furthering understanding but also seeking positive change.[7]

As we reflect on those themes of navigating a changing world, an ability to ask the right questions and develop knowledge to support a response seems of particular relevance.

Non-verbal Language

Language is not simply shared through words; it can be shared in other ways too. For those children for whom verbal communication is challenging, it can

---

[7] Powerful concepts such as children as 'first responders' and adults as 'co researchers' add to a vision for evolving research in schools both inside and outside of the classroom (Hume, 2023).

be really important to spend time exploring and reflecting on making the language for learning, discussed above, accessible. A non-verbal language, where necessary, offers a means for ensuring an ongoing commitment to a unified language that allows all to stay connected.[8]

3. GIVE IT A GO

Your Vocabulary

As you think about language you may wish to simply start reflecting on:

- What is the language for learning in your learning setting?
- Are there areas of practice where a technical language would make a difference? What and why?
- What resources or tools do you already use to support an accessible language for learning?

4. KEEP ON LEARNING…

> **Extending the Conversation …**
>
> Comedy is built on the confusions that can arise from misinterpretations with language. As well as this being funny, not speaking the right language can have paralysing learning consequences (Caslin et al., 2022).
>
> One challenge for lifelong learners is the ability to navigate between different vocabularies in different learning settings. It demands that those of us who facilitate learning find ways to ensure language does not act as a barrier. It demands we have a more open and widely recognised language that surrounds learning that is common to all.
>
> Think more about how 'clean language' might help to inform a shift in your practices – see the link below.
>
> https://cleanlearning.co.uk/blog/discuss/reflection-in-education

---

[8] An interesting discussion on 'voice' in a non-verbal setting – see Turner, 2018.

9

'G' – GROW MEANINGFUL OPPORTUNITIES

A marked shift in a 'learnt to be' as opposed to a 'taught to become' culture is the invitation for learners to have a sense that their engagement matters. A commitment to participation not only has benefits for the role learners can then play in shaping the culture for learning, but it also leads to the learning encounters themselves becoming increasingly meaningful. If adults hold restricted understanding of participation, it limits the meaningfulness of the opportunity that can be created (Alderson & Morrow, 2011), with an impact on the nature of the experience that the learner has. Let's revisit 'an opportunity' and reflect on how its design can support the learner to connect, with relevance for building an environment focused on learning as navigation and learning by consent.

1. HAVE AN IDEA

Questions: Value, voice and vision thrive off meaningful opportunities – how meaningful are the opportunities you create?

2. TALK, LISTEN AND PLAN

Thinking About Opportunities

Launched in 2010 as part of the then Government's vision for a Big Society, the National Citizen Service aimed to provide opportunities for young people to find their place in society by 'graduating' from a series of activities that enabled them as 'citizens'. An analysis (Bacon et al., 2013) at the time of its inception highlighted five areas of concern over the way in which this national project was presented ...

(1) Does it (NCS) show enough respect for the competences children already have?
(2) Does it respond to the power imbalance that results in children's marginalisation?
(3) Are the activities centred on re-defining power relationships that would then enable children to actually be part of directing change in their communities?
(4) Does the project create a hierarchy of 'citizens' with those who attend being seen as more deserving than others (with little or no regard to other ways in which those others might be actively engaged in their communities)?
(5) What does the need for this project say about the other ways in which children are educated as citizens?

The series of questions offer a broader framework that we might apply to the nature of the opportunities around us. Indeed, without a foundation that

- acknowledges children's competence
- addresses undying issues of power
- values a variety of participative pathways
- connects with the existing curriculum meaningfulness is always going to be limited.

Similar concerns over 'meaningfulness' have been noted by other academics in relation to children and classroom based engagement. Weller summarises this by saying 'citizenship education is not only about creating future citizens, but also about institutionalising, controlling and shaping the kind of participation in which teenagers may legitimately engage' (2009, p. 20). It is a damning indictment, but one that can be firmly understood in the context of a 'taught to become' culture. The implications of this in the context of a changing world are, as Felissa Tibbitts (2017) notes, that traditional forms of teacher pupil engagement driven by adult directed pedagogies, continue to result in missed opportunities that limit a focus on empowerment, activism and transformation.

> *A central part of a culture of advocacy, that allows learners to connect is the need to create opportunities that are meaningful,*

> *not just in respect of one area of the curriculum but throughout a learning community, using the following actions as a guide...*

- Build opportunities that encourage
- Create opportunities that are relevant
- Design opportunities that empower
- Be ambitious in how these opportunities can offer change

Build Opportunities That Encourage

The Connected Learner is presented to challenge existing and pervasive ways of thinking about both the learner and learning. At the heart of our argument is a recognition of the capacity of the child as a meaning maker, as a socially active and engaged contributor to everyday interactions – a social agent in their own right. Research that we looked at in Chapter 5 found that children learn best when they feel known and understood and when they feel respected for whom they are. This requires commitment on the part of the adult.

Previous discussions have invited you to highlight 'value' as a component of the connected learner, enabled through activities that encourage a focus on:

- Self-confidence – an ability/willingness to share ideas, wants and needs
- Self-respect – a sense of who you are and what you stand for
- Self-esteem – what makes your social contribution unique - leading to feelings of self-worth

This takes us part of the way. For although, 'value' in oneself is necessary, it is connected to a wider goal for us to be part of a shared vision, where we seek to encourage not only our own abilities but the abilities of others. Alongside our sense of self, we also, therefore, need an awareness of the 'other',[1] and with it a desire to engage with...

- Other confidence
- Other respect
- Other esteem

---

[1] see Chapter 2 and the work of Jonathan Sachs (2020).

Learning opportunities that are developed in relation to ourselves as well as others can be assessed for efficacy through their planning, delivery and evaluation, where results are determined by the growth in a positive learning identity (value, voice and vision).

Create Opportunities That Are Relevant

A focus on learning as performance (see Chapter 4) means that the exchange of content (from the teacher to the pupil) becomes all important. The learner has a list of 'knowledge' they are expected to know as a basis on which they can then be assessed as successful (or not). But what if the aim of the activity was not simply about remembering but engaging with a wider process, where learners approach the task with a focus on their learning identities and their own personalised learning goals and objectives? John Hattie (2020) reflects on the debate over whether in the context of 'twenty-first century learning' – skill development rather than knowledge acquisition is the priority. Rather than seeing this as an either-or, but more a balance, creates ways in which related opportunities can be increasingly tailored to the individual as part of *their* learning journeys.

Alfie Kohn (2011) in his essay 'how to create nonreaders: reflections on motivation, learning and sharing power' adds to a discussion on relevance through the notion of autonomy. He recognises the power of schools to compel action – improving readers through – quantifying assignments, making them write reading reports and isolating them (and more). In contrast to inviting a 'desire to learn' through creating opportunities that focus on autonomy. This is presented in a collaborative sense, recognising the role that the adult might play in supporting choices, setting targets and guiding skill development. A sense of control adds to motivation as the opportunities become relevant in the context of that individual's learning experiences.

A consideration of relevance also allows us to think about widening the net of 'recognised' spaces within which a learning opportunity might take place. Part of the challenge within education has been the 'relevance' that has been attached to the formal curriculum and the spaces within which this is delivered. However, learning does not just take place in the classroom. If our focus is increasingly on the journey, then it opens up the scope to see learning in other spaces too.² Recognising the value of informal learning opportunities extends the relevance of every learning experience.

Design and Deliver Opportunities That Empower

Imposition largely negates opportunities. In the context of international development work in the 1960s and 1970s, the effectiveness of an intervention was reduced, if the measure was one that was developed by outsiders and 'dropped' on local people.

Imposing ideas in this way meant local people were disconnected; the ideas were not their own, they did not address the issues in the way they perceived them and ultimately the local people were reduced to 'objects' of an experiment delivered by a more powerful 'other'.

This is the opposite to empower. To be effective, research showed that local people needed to have agency

– recognising who owned the problem

– given the chance to talk and be listened to

– taken seriously

– seen as part of the solution – in shaping a response.

Described as 'bottom up', opportunities can be created that empower learners.³ Can curriculum design and aspects of children's experience of school represent a series of opportunities where the learner is involved in the shaping of the how, what, when, where and why of the learning programme. This approach is strongly reinforced by Paulo Freire (2021), who within the context of education encourages this shift from people as 'passive recipients of knowledge' to a 'problem posing' approach in which they become actively involved – empowered to participate. Empowering opportunities allows learners to connect their ambitions for the real world to what they do in the classroom, with a mind to find personal and community oriented solutions that are meaningful to them.

---

2 For example, outdoor learning.
3 White (1996) highlights four levels of engagement (i) Nominal participation – for display – top down (ii) Instrumental participation – focused on particular end, top down may consult (iii) Representative participation – bottom up, but driven by interests and focus of those at the top (iv) Transformational participation – participation both means and end for top and bottom – aim is empowerment.

Be Ambitious in How These Opportunities Can Offer Change

Being ambitious might include goals to bring about global change, but on a day to day level are more likely to involve specific conversations about setting and achieving personal bests. This invites us to move away from perceptions of achievement based on having to reach a certain mark in a particular test on a set date, allowing us to explore learning targets that recognise the progress of a learning journey. Goals or targets are part of the process, but these are personalised and set to boost a sense of achievement. Athletic coaching models, for example, talk about 'positive feedback loops' as a constant and necessary part of maintaining our connection, and building are ambition throughout a given task.

Be ambitious, encourages us to design opportunities in such a way that they further our ambitions, recognising process rather than simply destination. This allows us to position ourselves more confidently for taking risk and challenging ourselves further. Opening up space in which we can freely acknowledge aspects of learning that we find most challenging, allows us to set more meaningful ambitions for our learning journeys.

3. GIVE IT A GO

Think about some learning opportunities...

How and in what ways do these opportunities/or could these opportunities advance the learners vision to strengthen their learning identity? (Fig. 34)

	What is this learning opportunity?		
This opportunity/ platform...	How is this visible?	How might this be added to?	Your action steps
Encourages the individual			
Creates relevant experiences			
Empowers children as change makers			
Is *Ambitious* in scope and intended outcomes			

Fig. 34. What is a Learning Opportunity.

4. KEEP ON LEARNING

Extending the Conversation

Reflecting on the lifelong learner, particularly for those that have been out of learning for some time, it can be hard to identify and seize an opportunity. The fact is that learning opportunities are all around us. What I like about this story is how it reminds us of the everyday nature of learning, but also the way in which creating the right opportunity had such powerful results for everyone involved.

I was meeting with a group of parents at school. One mum talked about the challenges she had with her 6 year old son, Alfie. Every morning, she packed his school bag and was waiting at the front door when it was time to leave. And every day Alfie sat on the stairs and refused to leave the house. Every day she ended up losing her temper and shouting. Every day they walked to school without talking. It was damaging their relationship. She had always felt it was her job to 'know best' to act in ways that she thought was in the 'interests' of her child. Then one day she went on a course where she was asked - so what does your child think? So she came home and that day started a conversation. They talked and she listened. Alfie explained that he was anxious that he might be missing things he needed for school. He wanted to know what was in his bag. So mum changed the morning routine. She created a check list each night of the things she thought needed to be in the bag and each morning they checked the bag together. No more fights. Lots of chat on the way to school. A change in perspective, resulting in a conversation that transformed their relationship.

Think about the everyday opportunities you can create as you seek to build value, voice and vision.

10

'IN' – INSPIRE LEAD LEARNERS

In our review of Connected Learning in practice has made clear that in an effort to establish an environment in which a learner can effectively connect, demands a level of self-evaluation from the facilitator. In this chapter, we are keen to re-assert that, only when a 'teacher' has a strong sense of promoting positive learning identities will they be most effective. Facilitators are learners too! Within our ambitions for the 'connected learner' and that lifelong journey, the significance of what it means to 'keep on learning' is heightened, as instructors, facilitators, teachers are encouraged to engage with their place as a 'lead learner'.

In a recent collection of academic papers from around the world, a common theme that emerged amongst the educationalists was the value of professional reflection. Whether this was in relation to early years education (Frankel, 2022; 2023, OECD, 2023 – Starting Stong V1), or within the context of classroom engagement or outdoor learning, the value in taking time to review and evaluate ones practices was clear. An opportunity to reflect precedes a deeper agenda to inspire change. We encourage you to take that time and to recognise reflective practice within the broader goal of maximising learning connections.

We share some thoughts below hoping to trigger professional learning conversations, as we look at how your value, voice and vision matter too!

1. HAVE AN IDEA

Question: How does reflecting on our own value, voice and vision as learners boost the learning identities of others?

2. TALK, LISTEN AND PLAN

Reflecting on Value

Being a teacher is not a career chosen without some sense of vocation.

Kate Clancy (2019), author of Some Kids I Taught and What they Taught Me – says 'I started training to be a teacher…because I wanted to change the world…'

Writing in the Financial Times at the end of another pandemic lockdown in March 2021, Lucy Kellaway (2021) writes

> When I started out as a teacher, I thought it was my job to inspire. I wanted to teach my students about the real economy and real business. I wanted to prepare them for the world by telling them about it and interesting them in it.

However, the challenge for teachers is that feeling as though one can make that difference has been limited. Lucy Kellaway continues…

> Yet about a year ago, I stopped all that. The penny dropped: my view of education was at odds with the prevailing one. The point of education as currently configured is as a signalling device to universities and employers – students with the right exam scores are allowed on to the next phase of life. The children need the qualifications not to understand the world, but to make their way in it. The point of my job is to open the doors for students, and exams are those doors. That means under the current regime…I was doing my now students not a favour but a disservice.

That struggle to match a passion for making a difference, alongside the practicalities of what one is required to do in the classroom has created a crisis of confidence, that is reflected in the levels of those leaving the profession (Guardian 23/2/23) and the broader pressures the system creates (NEU, 2021; Guardian 31/12/22). Without a sense of one's own value, it is more challenging to promote the value of others. So how do teachers re-connect?

Within the context of 'allowing learning', our answer recognises the messiness that is involved in learning, and championing the way in which a connected learner navigates their way through. Robinson and Aronica (2016) talks about the level of complexity attached to the role of a 'teacher' with reference to the term 'facilitator'. He describes effective facilitation within the classroom as being 'an art' and a role of considerable challenge. It demands recognition of a level of expertise and a skill set that allows the adult to understand what each learner needs to further their learning identity. It is this that we want to champion, as a key component to a wider ambition for promoting the connected learner.

Reviewing the 'facilitator' in a little more detail, allows us to note the social orientation of the role and what this means for the relationship between the learner and facilitator. The facilitator sits alongside other terms such as 'coach'. Coaching emerged as a next step from 'instruction'. What Timothy Gallwey (1976, 1981) noted in his observations of tennis, golf and skiing was that the main barrier to your best performance (your personal best) was not the competition (who you were up against) but yourself, what is in your head. Coaching offered the chance to focus on those internal barriers to performance, where the role of the coach is to help the athlete (or in our case the learner) manage their thinking and take control of their performance. Blending coach with Robinson and Aronica (2016) vision of the skilled facilitator as an artist, seamlessly weaving together the right opportunities alongside needed content and skill development in ways that empower the learner to take control of their own performance, creates what we have termed elsewhere as the 'active coach' (Frankel, 2018a).

The active coach draws on a range of skills and levels of awareness that allows them to blend aspects of facilitation, coaching and knowledge expertise. It is a role that acknowledges the changing landscape and has the flexibility to adapt to being a champion for the promotion of those different components that make up the connected learner. Celebrating the teacher as an artist, allows investment in the application of the different tones and techniques that equip each learner to 'shine'. As confidence in their value increases, so it becomes more possible for the 'teacher' to project the art of learning to others. What is notable, from research on metacognition for example, is the significance of approaches such as conversations, modelling and clean language, that can be used to bring these 'navigation; skills to life.

> *The evidence suggests that a mix of approaches is necessary to effectively develop SRL (self regulated learning) and metacognitive knowledge and skills. Explicit teaching of strategies and teacher modelling, not least through verbalising while problem solving are an essential element of effective teaching in this area. However, in order to develop metacognitive reflection, it is also necessary to develop practise through dialogue and more open-ended, albeit guided, inquiry work in which pupils are given more autonomy*

> *over tasks within a framework of scaffolds, prompts and teacher guidance.*
>
> *(Muijs & Bokhove, 2020, p. 33)*

It is through taking value in the skills that sit around the 'art' of learning and navigating the messiness of a learning experience, that the teacher can fully demonstrate their value as a 'lead learner'. It is only with the confidence that comes from recognising ones value, that the teacher is in a position to create an environment that allows that social dimension to learning to become visible, whether that is in relation to learning vulnerabilities, managing collaboration or dealing with risk. Indeed, it is only when teachers are in a position to project their trust on the learner, that we know we have reached a point where connections are maximised. As John Hattie says…

> *…what is most important is that teaching is visible to the student, and that the learning is visible to the teacher. The more the student becomes the teacher and the more the teacher becomes the learner, then the more successful are the outcomes.*
>
> *(Hattie, 2009, p. 25 – see also 2012, p. 17)*

For a facilitator to value their expertise to manage, make sense and control the art of learning – contributes to the ability for learners within that environment to enhance their connections.

Reflecting on Voice

'Good relationships keep us healthier and happier. Period' (Waldinger & Shulz, 2023, p. 10). We have spoken about the use of 'voice' as a means to make a contribution and position oneself within a narrative. But, voice on its own does not make a relationship. For voice to be effective, someone needs to listen. It is in that coming together, that we suggest, we find not only a basis for stronger learning relationships (learning by consent) but also for expanding our capacity as a learner. Nancy Kline (2020) presents in her book, 'the promise that changes everything', that if we could improve our ability to listen, if we could 'stop interrupting', this would enable independent thinkers.

Klein offers some startlingly data on the average listening times of professional listeners, people paid to listen, including teachers. In 2017, she says this was only 20 seconds and rather than this getting any better since (despite increasing awareness around wellbeing) in 2020 the average amount of time given to listening to a client was 11 seconds. What Kline highlights is that we don't actually listen, rather we find ways to fill any silences and to direct conversations around to our own ways of thinking. So 'we interrupt – over and over again. All of us. Paid and not. Partners and parents. Leaders and learners' (2020, p. 8).

The consequence of our interruptions, as Kline argues, is that it 'diminishes' our thinking. It decreases our ability to develop our thoughts, limiting the value that we then attach to them. The result for Kline is that 'our decisions are weaker; our relationships are thinner' (2020, p. 8). The result 'we disconnect. Our thinking shrivels. And polarisation is born' (2020, p. 10).

For Kline, however, there is a solution – for us to be better listeners. Notably that listening needs to be genuine. She questions how often we have been asked the question 'what do you think' and have then felt someone has actually listened to the answer. For so many, she suggests, that has never been the case. It is through that encouragement of being listened to that our 'luminous core of intelligence' is able to be expressed, directly contributing to our sense of self and a positive learning identity. Kline identifies ten[1] components to support effective listening and enable a thinking environment. However, to establish a starting point and to foster this sense of a thinking space, we can simply begin by:

(1) Giving attention

(2) Staying interested

(3) Sharing the stage

As a result of this, independent thinking is triggered

> ...as we experience attention and know we will not be interrupted. It is the 'knowing', the promise, that produces the trust that produces the courage that produces our new thinking. (2020, p. 17)

A feature of 'independent thinking' is how it is rooted in an interdependent culture, so that there is a role to be played by both the learner and those around them in enabling the effective execution of this latent ability. It is a compelling argument that ties back into the themes from earlier around courage and how through listening and effective learning conversations, we can support the individual to further their sense of value, voice and vision.

---

1 Attention, Equality, Ease, Appreciation, Feelings, Encouragement, Information, Difference, Inclusive questions, Place.

Reflecting on Vision

Vision is the responsibility of the leader! So when you hear the term leader – where do you look? A leader, here, is someone different to the drill sergeant who shouts orders that others are expected to be follow. Today, models such as the 'charismatic leader' centre more on the need to inspire and motivate, which result in what is described as 'transformational and transactional leadership' (Nye, 2008). That focus on relationships shifts who we might look to as leaders, opening it up to 'all of us' to varying degrees, within the context of the different parts we play in our learning communities.

It is this social aspect of leadership, alongside those more recognised skills (such as empathy, risk management, adaptability),[2] that stand out within the context of this book. Indeed, it is in a courageous search to provide a structure through which change might be navigated that becomes particularly defining. In Chapter 2, we set out a model for this...

(1) Locate – know where we are

(2) Look – know where you want to go

(3) Lead – know how we make the move

It is through the scope to maximise opportunities through which a learner might make that shift on the connection continuum as they develop their sense of value, voice and vision, which makes the role of the teacher as leader so powerful.

In an interesting take on schools that recognises the challenges and contributions that indigenous learners have had – around vision, Linda Lantieri, talks about the need to make those connections between a child's sense of self, their identity and the learning space through being 'schools with spirit'

> ... *'schools with spirit [are] dedicated to all children who would benefit from having their inner lives more present in our classrooms and to the adults that have the courage to evoke that change'. (xi)*

Courage thus emerges as a basic quality for taking the lead and inspiring children as learners, through intentional learning encounters that further 'belonging, connectedness, meaning and purpose' (7). In challenging the idea of schools as 'giant test prep centres', she asks an intriguing question - 'if you could wake up one morning with the power to teach children one thing what

---

2 'Empathetic executives are more attuned to the needs of people around them. They are better at managing relationships and relating to others. They are more likely to establish trust, creating safer environments to work in. Empathy also facilitates collaboration' (de Vries, 2019, p. 131).

would it be?' (11). Their response, that learners are 'loved, have purpose, are tolerant and compassionate and that they have a sense of interconnectedness'. It is through the strength of relationships that trust is nurtured, enabling the adult to inspire a vision for those within that learning community (a group, class or school) to explore their 'inner lives' with courage and through this further their identities as learners.

3. GIVE IT A GO

Your Own Research

Plan your own Action Research – Using four apparently simple words will take you through an Active Learning Cycle: Do → Review → Learn → Apply (Dennison & Kirk, 1990). Applied at an individual level this brings understanding and new insights, applied as a whole team-it can lead to a process review of any activity.

Impact

To support an assessment of the impact that you are having - consider the following model that highlights the 'ripple' effect of your actions... (Fig. 35).

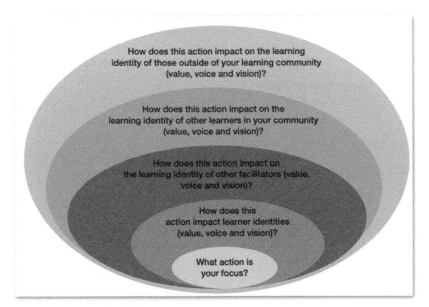

Fig. 35. The Ripple Effect.

Plan your own piece of appreciative enquiry to extend the part you play in leading change!

4. KEEP ON LEARNING...

> **Extending the Conversation**
>
> We should all recognise in ourselves our capacity to be 'lead learners'. Being a lead learner requires confidence in your own learning identity and positive experiences that allow you to nurture your sense of value, voice and vision. An ability to inspire lifelong learning rests in the ambition of those who share that vision. So let passion define you're learning identity and through that inspire others.
>
> How do questions like the following support your reflections on being a lead learner? (Fig. 36)

Situational Awareness	Where are you and where do you want to go?
Empathy	How aware are you of your own feelings and those of others?
Inquiry	How have you created an atmosphere of curiosity and investigation?
Dialogue	What are the critical conversations you need to start?
Adaptability/ Flexibility	How do you enable a community response to challenges or changes in direction?
Risk Taking	How do you value risk and evaluate and measure learning experiences?

Fig. 36. Leadership Attributes.

11

THE INDIVIDUAL AS A CONNECTED LEARNER

> *Life ultimately means taking the responsibility to find the right answers to its problems and to fulfil the tasks which it constantly sets for each individual.*
>
> *(Frankl & Viktor, 2004, p. 85)*

How we respond to those questions that we raised back in Chapter 2

i. Who is a learner?

ii. What is learning for?

iii. How can we allow learning?

will define our ability to navigate our own learning environments and adapt to some of the current changes that the world is facing (Fig. 37).

Chapters 3–5 have shown how contrasting positions of thought can lead to very different responses to these questions. We have seen that how we think about these wider issues shapes our attitudes that drive the practices we create for learning but they also inform how we see ourselves as learners – our learning identities. Through these chapters, we have suggested that ourselves as learners – our learning identity – reflects a continuum that extends between connection and disconnection. Although a sense of disconnection can be pervasive and distort our ability to be positive, for example, the learner who says 'I am rubbish at art...', what we have shown is that it need not be defining. Our ambition has been to awaken an awareness of the *connected*

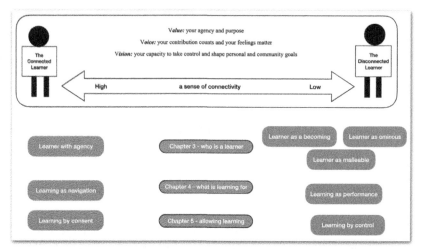

Fig. 37. Chapter Overview.

learner and the possibilities for making a 'shift' that allows us to establish, restore and maintain a high level of learning connectivity. It moves us from 'I am rubbish at art...' towards 'Wow look at all these colours, this is how I could match them'. To make this shift, we have to invest in ourselves, recognising our value, voice and vision.

SWITCH ON – ACTIVATING YOUR LEARNING CAPABILITIES

One way of becoming more connected to your learning is to look through the prism of the different dimensions that inform that learning. 'Meta-learning' refers to a range of dimensions, which reflect relationships, feelings and emotions, ambitions and goals and of course the context within which learning happens (Watkins et al., 2007, p. 123). It is an awareness of these interrelated dimensions that inform a learning experience that is at the centre of being a connected learner. In practical terms, this means an acknowledgement of

(1) My learning potential – I am a learner with agency

(2) Making my learning visible – navigate my learning

(3) Being me – my feelings and emotions

(4) My learning journey – exploring my learning possibilities

The Individual as a Connected Learner   143

Switching on your capacity to learn links to these four different but interconnected dimensions of a learning experience.

The format that we used in the last chapters bears repeating here

- Have an Idea

- Talk, Listen and Plan

- Give It a Go

- Keep on Learning

as we start to tease out the importance of exploring these aspects of the internal capability of the learner noted above. It is not our aim here to develop these in full, but merely to make the link with ideas shared previously and to highlight the possibilities of where our research needs to be directed next.

MY LEARNING POTENTIAL – I AM A LEARNER WITH AGENCY

1. Have an Idea

Question: How do you make learning potential a focus of attention for the learner?

2. Talk, Listen and Plan

We set out the contrasting positions around how we see ourselves as learners in Chapter 3 (Fig. 38).

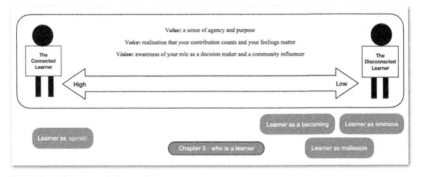

Fig. 38. Chapter 3 Overview.

Attitudes and assumptions have informed the learning landscape that then allows the 'disconnected learner' to thrive, shaping practices and distorting experiences. The learner's potential is, reduced to an image of a 'blank slate', passively waiting to be filled by the omnipotent teacher. However, this was in marked contrast to the learner with agency, where the individual's capacity to make meaning is seen as active and present – a function of their everyday lives. It is this active sense of the child as a learner (with application to learners of other ages too) that educational reformer John Dewey, writing in the first half of the twentieth century, acknowledges in offering his take on learning 'potential'.[1] For example, Dewey in a discussion about 'growth' says, 'growth is not something done to them [children]; it is something they do' (2011, p. 26). This forms part of a wider argument where Dewey is inviting his reader to understand the positive nature of immaturity as he suggests it should not simply be seen (as in the thinking above) as filling a void. He specifically highlights the terms 'capacity' and 'potentiality' and argues that both, in adult centric thinking, can be seen as carrying a negative connotation – capability is about the receptiveness of the child and potentiality is their capacity to be changed as a result of the external forces employed around them. He stresses an alternative where...

– capacity is seen as 'an ability, a power' (2011, p. 26) and

– potentiality becomes about 'potency, force'.

both of which, re-emphasise the place of the individual at the centre of their learning (Fig. 39).

	The Disconnected Learner	The Connected Learner
Capacity	The receptiveness of the child (learner) to adult (teacher) instruction	A tapped or untapped ability
Potentiality	A plasticity to be changed as a result of adult (treacher) interventions	An inner strength (the power to give it a go)

Fig. 39. Capacity and Potentiality.

Dewey's thinking reflects the paradigm shift that has been at the centre of this book as we consider how to re-imagine learners. Notably, being a 'connected learner' includes an active reflection on our own capability and potential. This dynamic and purposeful notion of ability and inner strength supports Carol Dweck's research on mindset (2016) as we recognise that 'the view you adopt for yourself profoundly affects the way you live your life'

---

[1] Could say something about the limited way in which Dewey's views took hold.

(Dweck, 2016, p. 11). If we can have a growth mindset, recognising your potential – you can move beyond what you might have originally labelled 'impossible' and re-categorise it as 'possible', it marks the ability to 'shift' between the disconnected and the connected learner.

3. Give It a Go

This highlights the importance of explicit conversations focused on awakening a realisation of the potential that we *all* have as learners. It invites questions and requires facilitators take time to talk to learners about their learning identity and their value, voice and vision.

Start the conversation with a simple activity like the one below – create a focus of attention on which you can build.

Create a space through which the learner (as apprentice[2]) can be actively engaged in exploring that sense of self through the following task (Fig. 40).

(1) Invite learners to spend a moment thinking about 'skills they have'[3] – apply to this learning journey.

(2) Invite learners to spend a moment thinking about 'skills they wish to develop' – on this learning journey.

(3) Discuss

(4) Complete learning journey

(5) Return to the skills identified and reflect on how they were used, how they were developed.

---

[2] Barbara Rogoff builds a model for learning that centres on releasing the potential of the individual. It is called 'guided participation', where learning happens as a process of interactions 'information and skills are not transmitted but are transferred in the process of appropriation...as individuals participate in social activity, they choose some aspects for attention and ignore others and they transform what is available to fit their uses' (1990, p. 197). As such children are to be seen as apprentices 'active in their efforts to learn from observing and participating with their peers and more skilled members of society' (1990, p. 7).

[3] Muijs and Bokhove (2020, p. 12) offer a list of example attributes. Also see Lucas and Spencer's description of capabilities (2020, p. 5).

Fig. 40. Exploring Your Skills.

An adaptation of this activity asks us to think about our inner selves and identifies how we might be disconnected.

(1) Draw a picture of yourself

(2) Inside write how you see yourself in relation to the task

(3) Outside write how you think others see you in relation to the task

Complete this activity by assessing your perceptions, at the beginning remember to include limiting thoughts. Do the same at the end of the activity. How did you help yourself, what did you need to challenge?

4. Keep on Learning...

Extending the Conversation

Take a look at the following model that outlines – 'meta learning'. Reflect on its application within the context of your learning setting.

Meta Learning Process

Do...the activity

Review the learning

> purpose
> strategy
> effects and outcomes
> emotions
>
> *Learn about the links to your learning*
>
> related to:
> purpose
> strategy
> effects and outcomes
> emotions
>
> *Apply to future learning*
>
> Your next:
> Purpose
> Strategy
> Effects and outcomes
> Managing Emotions
>
> (Adapted from Watkins et al., 2000)

MAKING MY LEARNING VISIBLE – NAVIGATE MY LEARNING

1. Have an Idea

Question: What are the points of the compass that you use to navigate your learning?

2. Talk, Listen and Plan

Chapter 4 looked at a vision for learning that emerged in response to significant social and technological change over 150 years ago – compulsory schooling. It emphasised a model where standardisation was key, as learning, alongside the wider industrial economy, centred on increased productivity. The learner became a cog in a much bigger wheel, where their value lies in the contribution they make to the workplace. Through a process of testing – learning becomes a means to position those resources appropriately – via exams we find our way into particular jobs. This focus on performance and knowledge has hidden our wider potential. In a world where knowledge is everywhere, the skills and strategies we use to manage that knowledge become increasingly important (Fig. 41).

Fig. 41. Chapter 4 Overview.

It might seem obvious that for a learning journey to be effective we need to have a sense of where we are, where we want to go and what steps we need to get there – but this is an aspect of learning that is too often assumed and not fully considered. It is also an aspect of learning that, if we doubt our ability, can quickly lead us into a downward spiral where feeling out of control, 'I can't do this', can result in a loss of confidence and 'disconnection'.

A number of commentators have pointed out that learning is not a frequent topic of conversations in schools. We have often noticed in our chats with teachers and children the steps involved in learning, are at best assumed at worst not understood or acknowledged. It is a realisation of this void that John Hattie's call for us to 'make learning visible' (Hattie, 2009) offers such an important contribution. We visited the detail behind this in Chapter 4. Part of this included introducing our four headings, revisited at the beginning of this chapter that emerge as points of a compass that can help to navigate a learning journey, namely 'have an idea', 'talk, listen and plan', 'give it a go' and 'keep on learning'.

3. Give It a Go

We have set out some further thinking about these headings below to give you a sense of how these can be applied in a practical setting. We know how these work as an individual guide for learning, a group tool to shape and direct a learning task and as a planning framework. Here we introduce some of the thinking behind the headings to allow you to consider how these could be used to enable learners to navigate their learning journeys.

(i) *Have an Idea*

   a. *Key Questions:* What is your challenge, task(s), problem to solve or idea?

   b. *Make Visible: The 'ask'* the focus of your learning journey
   In order to be able to put a strategy into action – the learner first needs to know what the task is. Although this might not mean knowing the destination, it is important to have a sense of what the journey is all about so the learner knows what they are stepping into. The task itself might be chosen by another or it might be a task that the learner has decided on. Noting themes from our discussion about meaningful opportunities, reflecting on how a task comes to be set and how this is perceived by the learner can be significant in relation to task ownership and their connection to the activity.

   Having a section like 'Have an Idea' encourages learners to seek clarity on the task set. Is this task to gain an understanding of why volcanoes erupt or is the journey about 'developing questions' and 'identifying resources' to find out more about this topic? 'Have an Idea' gives learners and adults the chance to define what the task is, to answer core questions such as – is there a point, a purpose to this task for me – is it relevant? Without this focus, the learner is always going to struggle to connect.

   Clean Language Example: It looks like you are really into that task – what are you doing?
   Is there anything else about it (...)?

(ii) *Talk, Listen and Plan:*

   a. *Key Questions:* I know? We know? Plan of Action?

I Know? – supports a review process, allowing the learner to look through internal databases of information in search of what might be needed in the current activity. Not only is it about identifying previously used information (knowledge, skills or strategies), or information that has been recently considered, but also about exploring where any gaps might be.

We Know? – having had the chance to draw on one's own personal database of knowledge, we can then think about how useful it might be to draw on the databases of others. This encourages a consideration of the right kind of questions that will allow us to fill in the gaps, as well as to know where we might look (from people to books, to the internet).

Plan of Action: having reviewed the above, the learner is then in a great position to define the steps that will allow them to advance their journey. Being able to detail the plan allows the learner to break a journey down into manageable phases that can be reviewed and reflected on as they go.
In map form – this allows the learner to state

- what their starting point is
- where they want to go (breaking the journey into achievable phases)
- what they need to do to move to the next stage of their journey
- Milestones or review points that allow a pause moment when they can reflect back, check where they are at and whether they are heading in the right direction!

    b. *Make Visible:*

- the knowledge/skills and strategies you already have
- the knowledge/skills and strategies others have
- the steps to advance this learning journey

'Planning' is a term commonly used to define this part of the metacognitive process. In order to stress the social dimension, here, this is framed in relation to learning conversations with oneself or others on the way to creating a plan of action.

(iii) *Give It a Go*

    a. *Key Question:* ready to test run?

    b. *Make Visible:* your plan in practice

'Give it a go' is very much about just doing that – giving it a go! In order to further the experience, it is important to have an 'experience' to further, therefore, there needs to be some activity on which you can reflect. Although there are a number of aspects that could be assessed and reviewed, it is important to give a plan a chance, to get stuck in, get messy and see where it all leads.

Establishing the freedom for the individual learner to feel as though it is okay to experiment and to make 'mistakes' is an important part of 'testing a plan' – having a safe space for innovation, encouraging risks and stepping outside of a comfort zone.

(iv) *Keep on Learning*

    a. *Key Questions: Findings? Reflections?, Another go?, Share?, Apply?*

Findings? *Findings* – invites the learner to define a moment within the learning journey. As noted above, this could be a micro element that is zoomed in on, or could be a broader part of the experience.

Reflections? *Reflect and Review* – having a sense of the what you found one can then look back to the 'plan of action' and think a little more about how the journey has gone and whether it has advanced your ability to respond to the tasks set at the beginning.

Another go? *Another go* – do you need to repeat/change anything to achieve the goal?

Share? *Share* – how/where might it be relevant to share this learning as a record of achievement/to help others?

Apply? *Apply* – where can you apply this learning so it has future impact?

    b. *Make Visible:*

- Your reflections on
- Your plan in action
- What you discovered
- How your discoveries link to the journey you are on
- How your learning can be applied (elsewhere)
  The metacognitive process or that wider meta-learning (set out above) centres on reflection. 'Learning about your learning', therefore, encourages the learner to engage with those different dimensions of learning, thinking through their journey without feeling trapped or judged or that there is 'only one way to do it'.

This model allows us to look beyond fixed and sequential patterns of learning, allowing us to (re)orientate ourselves when we jump from one part of the process to another or find ourselves sidestepping or taking a detour.

4. Keep on Learning

> **Extending the Conversation**
>
> When we discuss 'keep on learning', it allows us to consider how recording a learning experience might benefit future learning. This ability to store up learning experiences to be able to use in the future is of real value. It raises questions about how we can do this effectively within the context of a subject topic - subject/topic and a school year, creating opportunities to look back. We need to be open to resources that allow us to look across learning tasks and apply strategies that cross boundaries and link the experiences we have in different contexts and at different times. An ability to be allowed to learn across such boundaries and to make connections will enable our learning in its fullest sense.

BEING ME – MANAGING MY FEELINGS AND EMOTIONS

1. Have an Idea

Questions: How do you take your 'learning temperature' and stay in tune with your feelings?

What is the value of a well-being thermometer?

2. Talk, Listen and Plan

Chapter 5 highlighted how feelings and emotions are a filter for understanding our learning connectivity (Fig. 42).

The Individual as a Connected Learner　　153

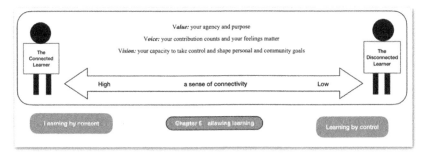

Fig. 42. Chapter 5 Overview.

No learning experience takes place in an emotional vacuum. Chapter 5 set out in detail that throughout any learning experience we will be feeling something, which will in turn have an impact on how we come to make sense of that learning encounter – informing our identity as a learner at that point in time. As we saw in Chapter 5, the way we perceive our relationships, shaped by our feelings, can be influential in framing a sense of mutuality and consent that can positively frame a learning experience. Sometimes emotions will be neutral and at other times they may be heightened (for example, with excitement or disappointment), how we respond or manage these emotions will influence how we learn and the knowledge we create.

Recognising that learning is part of you, brings with it the understanding that feelings and emotions are part of 'connecting'. 'Which side of the bed did you get out of today' might mean you are tired, disgruntled or annoyed, or alternatively you see the sun shining and you are inspired, energised and motivated. Such reflections impact our learning connectivity, our engagement and how we see ourselves as a learner!

3. Give It a Go

We discussed in Chapter 5 filters that inform our sense of self, as well as drawing on themes on identity formation shared throughout the book. Make a 'well-being thermometer' a focus for conversation as you assess your own learning connections. Taking time to reflect on how we are feeling can help us to focus on the learning encounter and the impact it is having on us.

The well-being thermometer
Reflective Question One – how do I feel?

As part of encouraging a deeper sense of reflection and conversation around feelings and emotions, we use non-specific emojis (Fig. 43).

Fig. 43. How Do I Feel Emoji.

This encouraged deeper reflections and created opportunities for conversations as the learners considered the nature of their feelings and how and why they might relate to the images.

Reflective Question Two – why do I feel like this?

The questions below provide triggers for conversations that can be used at varying levels, a quick chat, to a one-to-one intervention. The following table offers some prompts to explore the reasons that sit behind our feelings. These are simply conversation starters but each has the potential to inform a far deeper interrogation of past experiences and how these shape our meaning making (the way we associate feelings with a situation – through to how we see ourselves) (Fig. 44).

I feel the way I do because…			
Power	My sense of power means…	Being here?	This space **makes me feel**…
		Desire to succeed?	My ambition…
		Right and wrong?	What I know about right and wrong…
Body	My feelings of belonging mean…	Others?	The people around me…
		Me?	How I think about me…
		Your group?	The people I am learning with…
Capital	My desire to succeed means…	Knowledge and experience:	What I know…
		Tools and skills:	I have or I need and …

Fig. 44. Exploring Your Feelings.

4. Keep on Learning

> **Extending the Conversation**
>
> As part of exploring emotions, return to our conversation on clean language (Chapter 8), how might this help you to encourage others to manage their feelings?
>
> Engaging with our emotions can be harder for some than others. Watch Brené Brown's 2010 TED Talk (TED, 2010) or her Netflix documentary 'the call to courage' (Restrepo, 2019), how might her ideas on courage and vulnerability add to the way we enable learners to 'switch on' and be who they are?

MY LEARNING JOURNEY – EXPLORING MY LEARNING POSSIBILITIES

1. Have an Idea

Question: What possibilities can you see to advance your learning?

2. Talk, Listen and Plan

Realising our potential, managing our own learning journey, being in tune with our feelings and emotions, results in an opening out of possibilities.

Flow, which we looked at in Chapters 2 and 4, happens when everything comes together; when our use of past knowledge, skills and strategies are automatically integrated into our performance of a current task. Our desire to 'explore' should encourage us to recognise that a sense of 'flow' needs to have the edge of challenge. In considering Csikszentmihalyi (1997) notions of 'flow', Lucas and Spencer (2020) in their work 'zest for learning' remind us of the need for caution in thinking that when we are in 'flow' that is the best time to learn. For 'flow' might simply reflect an expression of muscle memory (they use the example of playing a piece of the piano that you have played many times before) – the act feels good, we are engaged but it is not allowing you to create new knowledge. For us, the positivity of being in flow as a basis for creating new knowledge should not be underestimated. It encourages us to be open to connections between those moments when we are in flow, and the learning opportunities this might create to extend our ambitions as we build on the positive feelings created by performing well.

Such opportunities means we are willing to look beyond what we know 'we can do', and open ourselves up to what we know 'we can't do yet'. It is about examining where our limits are and recognising those as temporal and porous, and a marker of a given time, not of a fixed ability. A search for possibilities demands we embrace risk, acknowledging our vulnerabilities as learners as an important, relevant and visible part of our own learning journeys. The fixed mindset (of Dweck, 2016) rejects the potential risk to the individual's learning identity that is posed by opening oneself up to tasks that might see them dislodged from whatever pedestal they have placed their learning identity on. 'Smart' is defined by being flawless and not making mistakes, approaching only tasks that they know to be 'possible'. This is in contrast to those with a growth mindset where the challenge provides an invitation to further oneself and extend ones capabilities – it becomes an opportunity for 'learning'. It is in the 'challenge' that those with a growth mindset thrive, as they are willing to explore what once might have been labelled 'impossible'.

Rather than risk being something that could damage our sense of self as a learner, we need to learn to 'explore' risk as a focus for expanding our vision for what is possible. As connected learners, we need to be more open about our learning vulnerabilities recognising these as a constant and regular part of our individual learning journeys[4] and acknowledge how these inform the way we might think about learning possibilities.

Exploring 'possibilities' as an active and definable element of our learning journeys encourages us to be objective as we stand back and see our learning journeys as a whole. It should allow us to take the 'long view' as we situate ourselves in our wider ambitions – the key is to make this part of our learning conversations!

3. Give It a Go

In order to visualise possibilities, it is important to try and capture your place in your learning journey. Over a period of time, have a go at recording your learning in a journal. Set some key dates and ask yourself the following questions as an observer – stepping back and looking at the big picture...

Locate – where are you

Look – where are you going

Leap – how are you going to get there

---

[4] It also allows us to extend narratives that swirl around the label of the 'disadvantaged learner', as we look for more personal solutions-based examining disadvantages.

- Keep the questions broad and open and use them to think about 'you' and 'your journey' and finding paths that are meaningful for you.
- In between these key dates you can always use the headings to reflect on specific 'sprints' of learning as you take on a particular task and record your experience!
- As a practical tool to get people thinking about possibilities, you may find it helpful to present some 'possibilities' to support them in engaging with a learning task – see the SOLUTIONS table in Fig. 45.

S	peak out	Who could you start a conversation with?
O	rangise differently	Who is part of the group? Could you change the roles? Draw on some different skills?
L	isten	Who could you hear from? Who has an opinion that might help?
U	nderstand more	What additional information might inform you better?
T	ime out	Would there be value in taking a break and step back and refresh your perspective?
I	magine and be confident	How might your creativity offer a response...?
O	ne more go, keep trying	Have you reflected on progress? Are you moving forward? Is there value in another go or is it time to revisit the learning compass?
N	egotiate	How does putting yourselves in the shoes of those you are learning with help you to consider their point of view? Does this help you to identify a plan that allows you all to move forward? What needs to happen for you to be a team?
S	earch and find	Where are you? Where do you want to go? What do you need to get there?
S	ome other strategies	What else would help to advance your vision?

Fig. 45. Exploring Solutions.

4. Keep on Learning

> **Extending the Conversation**
>
> *It is important not to underestimate the extent to which risk impacts on learning identities. As one friend shared – take a group of university learners... one group keeps asking questions and another group is just chatting away. The group that asks questions are making themselves vulnerable but they are able to make progress on the task. The group that keeps chatting are scared of admitting that*

they don't know the answer. They don't want to risk putting themselves in a space where 'asking a question' demands they admit to themselves they are not as 'good' a learner as they thought they were. One group has a growth mindset made visible by their willingness to take a risk, the other does not!

Reflect on an encounter where taking risk did or could have transformed the possibilities for one of your learning experiences.

12

ENDURING CONNECTIONS – LEARNING ALLOWED

The beautiful thing about learning is that nobody can take it away from you.

–B.B. King

The extract below was written over 15 years ago.

> *...the person is seen living at the centre of a web of relationships and contexts, and learning is seen as fundamentally social, the means by which people join communities and become who they aim to be. Here the personal is necessarily social and the person is seen as developing through interaction with others. So the process of personalisation is about building participation through belonging and collaboration, so that learning advances the collective knowledge and, in that way, supports the growth of individual knowledge. Key processes of interpretation, interaction and interdependence are promoted, and these contribute to becoming fully human.*
>
> *(Watkins, 2006, p. 5)*

It reflects the place of the individual as the creator and instigator of their learning journeys, engaged in processes that reflect and underpin what it means to be human. Many of the ideas we have shared are already out there, but disconnected. It is through 'connecting' them to drive how we 'enable learning' and how we are 'enabled to learn' that creates a paradigm shift. This shift centres on a recognition of becoming learners with agency, whose value, voice and vision deepens as we create knowledge by making sense of our learning experiences across different times and different spaces. We want you, and those you learn with, to re-imagine your learner identities as part of what it means to be *you* and for this to extend our shared passion to make 'learning allowed', by focusing on strengthening our learning connectivity within *all* communities.

Chapter 1 explained why this conversation is urgent. Fig. 24 represents the growth of a connected learner, possessing a positive sense of their learning identity. By connecting with *their full* capabilities a learner is able to drive a process that connects them with others, increasing societies' capacity as a whole to navigate change and find solutions (Fig. 46).

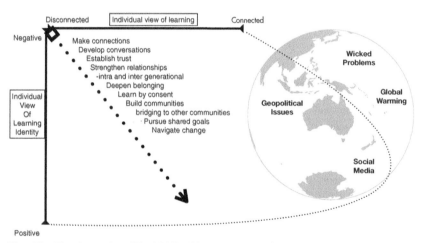

Fig. 46. The Learning World We Would Like to See.

LET'S CHANGE THE NARRATIVE

Striving to be a connected learner is no simple option. It is complex and fluid, marking a process of identity formation that is constant and ongoing. It involves enabling the learner to expand their capabilities as they learn from the many and varied opportunities that form part of their everyday lives. It requires that both a learner and facilitator have to want to 'allow' learning. This is not a question of permission, rather one of intention. Key, therefore, to the connected learner, is a willingness to make our learning identities a focus of attention, as we constantly ask ourselves and others where we are positioned on that 'connection' continuum.

Chapter 2 told the story of Jack, who was an inspiration for some of our thinking. Jack opened our eyes to a world in which identities of disconnection are very real when one lacks a sense of value, voice and vision. However, he showed us that such an identity is not fixed but can change, as connections are made and then given the chance to deepen. If we were to imagine Jack's story as a film, he would be shown pursuing a range of learning ambitions off into the sunset, but the last we knew of Jack was not this happy ending. Sadly the transition to secondary school did not reinforce gains made in primary school, instead Jack returned to playing a part that he knew well - the disconnected learner. It is this aspect of Jack's story that continues to inspire us to seek change. Jack found himself up against a system where he was outplayed by institutional attitudes and practices that limited his ability to embody his capabilities as a learner.

If we are to respond to Jack's story we must be aware of the prevalence of discourses that impact our attitudes, our practices and as a result the experiences of those we encounter. All of us are constantly assessing our value, voice and vision, *even when we don't have the freedom to practice* them. This, realisation helps us to understand why assumptions that surround us, the becoming, ominous and malleable learner (from Chapter 3) are so damaging. We can change the narrative, the story we are able to re-tell, when we start to embrace the 'learner with agency'.

As we consider the learning environment, and the role we might play to enable a learner to 'plug in', we find ourselves questioning traditional approaches based on performance and begin to recognise the need for a focus on 'learning as navigation' (Chapter 4). As well as positive implications for learner connectivity, it also allows a focus on those capabilities that are needed as a response to current and future global change. From equipping learners to discern truth from conspiracy and lies, to a greater investment in emotional intelligence and interpersonal skills, through to recognising our capacity as change makers, the connected learner offers an identity that is meaningful and enduring.

Ours is an approach that requires compliance and obedience give way to a sense of mutuality, trust and equal power, where 'learning is by consent', framed within communities that share a common goal. 'One size fits all' no longer has a place, as we recognise the individual nature of our unique and varied learning journeys. As we stated in Chapter 5, it is through an investment in relationships built on accepting that we are known and understood, that we are able to maximise our learning.

It is unrealistic to expect people to always feel positive about learning, we all check out from time to time, but this approach is about establishing enough resilience in our sense of identity as learners that any break in 'connection' is temporary; we remain hungry to learn and are well equipped to carry out the necessary repairs. Throughout, and particularly in Chapter 6 to 11, we have contrasted current practice with our hope for the new. That 'hope' rests in you and your willingness to be intentional about making the connected learner a focus for your everyday learning and your practice. It is not as daunting as it seems, for if we remember that 'learning is being you', then to release that hope, all we need to do is awaken the connected learner in all of us, hence Learning Allowed...

> *We want learning to be allowed when ever, who ever, where ever we are – no ages or stages – creating positive learning identities and enduring connections to navigate our changing world.*

Together, let's extend this conversation!

REFERENCES

AARP https://youtu.be/lYdNjrUa1NM

Abc7. (2017, April 24). Former president Obama speaks at University of Chicago. http://abc7chicago.com/news/former-president-obama-speaks-at-u-of-c/1910280/. Accessed on October 3, 2017.

Alderson, P., & Morrow, V. (2011). *The ethics of research with children and young people: A practical handbook* (2nd ed.). SAGE.

Amos, H., & Laing, A. (1979). *These were the Greeks*. Stanley Thornes.

Archard, D. (2004). *Children: Rights and childhood*. Routledge.

Arthur, J. (Ed.). (2010). *Citizens of character: New directions in citizenship and values education*. Imprint Academic.

Bacon, K., & Frankel, S. (2013). 'Rethinking children's citizenship: Negotiating structure, shaping meanings. *The International Journal of Children's Rights*, 22(1), 21–42.

Bacon, K., Frankel, S., & Faulks, K. (2013). Building the 'Big Society': Exploring representations of young people and citizenship in the National Citizen Service. *The International Journal of Children's Rights*, 21, 1–22.

BBC News. (2023, February 13). Parents priest over Stoke on Trent school 'toilet ban'. https://www.bbc.co.uk/news/uk-england-stoke-staffordshire-64627138

BBC News. (2023, February 21). Firms stick to four-day week after trial ends. https://www.bbc.co.uk/news/business-64669987

Bluebond-Langner, M. (1978). *The private world of dying children*. Princeton University Press.

Bourdieu, P. (1990). *The logic of practice*. Polity.

Brooker, L. (2002). *Starting school – Young children learning cultures*. Open University Press.

Brooks, D. (2012). *The social animal: The hidden sources of love, character, and achievement* Random House *trade pbk. edn.* Random House Trade Paperbacks.

Burman, E. (1994). *Deconstructing developmental psychology*. Routledge.

Burnyeat, M. (1980). Aristotle on learning to be good. In A. Rorty (Ed.), *Essays on Aristotle's Ethics*. University of California Press.

Business Balls. (2023). https://www.businessballs.com/communication-skills/clean-language-david-grove-questioning-method/#clean-language-david-grove-questioning-method

Cairns-Lee, H., et al. (2022). In H. Cairns-Lee et al. (Ed.), *Clean language interviewing: Principles and applications for researchers*. Emerald Publishing Limited.

Cambridge Assessment International Education. (2023). https://cambridge-community.org.uk/professional-development/gswmeta/index.html

Caslin, M., Georgiou, H., Davies, C., & Spoor, S. (2022). No laughing matter. In S. Frankel (Ed.), *Establishing Child Centred Practice in a Changing World – Part A*. Emerald Publishing Limited.

Children and Young People Now. (2022). https://www.cypnow.co.uk/news/article/primary-school-attainment-gap-widest-in-a-decade

Children Count The Shinning Recorders of Zisize. http://childrencount.uct.ac.za/radio/index.php

Christie, N. (1977). Conflicts as property. *British Journal of Criminology, 17*(1), 1–15.

Clancy, K. (2019). *Some kids I taught and what they taught me*. Picador.

Claremont Graduate University. (2023). https://www.cgu.edu/people/mihaly-csikszentmihalyi/

Claxton, G., Chambers, M., Powell, G., & Lucas, B. (2011). *The learning powered school: Pioneering 21st century education*. TLO Limited.

Cockburn, T. (2013). *Rethinking Children's citizenship*. Palgrave Macmillan.

Cohen, A. P. (Ed.). (1982). *Belonging: Identity and social organisation in British rural cultures*. Manchester University Press.

Connolly, P. (1998). *Racism, gender identities and young children: Social relations in a multi ethnic, inner city primary school*. Routledge.

Connolly, P. (2004). *Boys and schooling in the early years*. Routledge Falmer.

Connolly, P. (2006). The masculine habitus as distributed cognition: A case study of 5- to 6-year-old boys in an English inner-city, multi-ethnic primary school. *Children & Society, 20*(2), 140–152.

Correia, N. (2023). Children's voice in early childhood education and care. In S. Frankel (Ed.), *Establishing Child Centred Practice in a Changing World – Part B*. Emerald Publishing Limited.

Cottam, H. (2018). *Radical help*. Virgo Press.

Crick, M. (1976). *Explorations in language and meaning*. Malaby Press.

Csikszentmihalyi, M. (1997). *Finding flow: The psychology of engagement with everyday life* (1st ed.). Basic Books.

Curtis, S., & Boultwood, M. (1977). *A short history of educational ideas*. University Tutorial Press.

Cussianovich, A. (2001). What does protagonism mean? In M. B. LiebelOverwien & A. Recknagel (Eds.), *Working Children's Protagonism: Social Movements and Empowerment in Latin America, Africa, and India* (pp. 157–169). IKO-Verlag für Interkulturelle Kommunikation.

Davies, L., Hunjan, R., & Lewis, S. M. (2005). Inspiring Schools Carnegie.

Deaken, J., Taylor, E., & Kupchik, A. (Eds.). (2018). *The Palgrave International Handbook of School Discipline, Surveillance, and Social Control*. Palgrave Macmillan.

Dennison, B., & Kirk, R. (1990). *Do review learn apply: A simple guide to experiential learning*. Nelson Thornes Ltd.

Department for Education. (2021). *Skills for jobs: Lifelong learning for opportunity and growth*. Crown Publishing.

Department for Education. (2022). *School recovery strategies*. Crown Publishing.

Dewey, J. (2011). *Democracy and education*. Simon and Brown.

Donaldson, M., & Hughes, M. (1979). The use of hiding games for the studying co-ordination of viewpoints. *Educational Review, 31*, 133–140.

Donaldson, M., & McGarrigle, J. (1975). Conversation Accidents. *Cognition, 3*, 34 1–50.

Douglas, M. (1966). *Purity and danger*. Routledge and Kegan.

Durkheim, E. (1951). *Suicide, a study in sociology*. Free Press.

Durkheim, E. (1978). *On institutional analysis*, M. Traugott (ed and trans). University of Chicago Press.

Dweck, C. S. (2016). *Mindset: The new psychology of success* (Updated edition). Ballantine Books.

Elkin, F. (1960). *Children and society: The process of socialisation*. Random House.

End Violence Against Children. (2022). http://www.endcorporalpunishment.org/wp-content/uploads/country-reports/UK.pdf

Equiano, O. (1789). *Sold as a slave*. Penguin.

EquippingKids. (2017). Research briefing 1: Seen and heard – Children's voices on school. EquippingKids. http://blog.equippingkids.org/2017/11/27/research-briefing-1-seen-and-heard-childrens-voices-on-school/

EquippingKids. (2018). Research briefing 2: Seen and heard – Children's voices on school. EquippingKids. https://www.equippingkids.org/news/our-latest-research-happiness-learning/

EquippingKids. (2022). Research briefing 3: Exploring learning at home and school. EquippingKids. https://www.equippingkids.org/media-hub-area/research-briefing-exploring-learning-at-home-school/

Fielding, M., & Moss, P. (2010). *Radical education and the common school*. Taylor and Francis Group.

Fletcher, A. (2008). *Growing up in England: The experience of childhood, 1600–1914*. Yale University Press.

Frankel, S. (2012). *Children, morality and society*. Palgrave Macmillan.

Frankel, S. (2017). *Negotiating childhoods*. Palgrave Macmillan.

Frankel, S. (2018a). *Giving children a voice: A step by step guide to promoting child centred practice*. Jessica Kingsley.

Frankel, S. (2018b). The art of belonging. (2018). In S. Frankel & S. McNamee (Eds.), *Contextualising Childhoods: Growing up in Europe and North America*. Palgrave Macmillan.

Frankel, S. (Ed.). (2022). *Establishing child centred practice in a changing world – Part A*. Emerald Publishing Limited.

Frankel, S. (Ed.). (2023). *Establishing child centred practice in a changing world – Part B*. Emerald Publishing Limited.

Frankel, S., & Fowler, J. (2016). *How to take your school on a journey to outstanding: Five building blocks to maximise children's social learning potential*. EquippingKids.

Frankel, S., & McNamee, S. (Eds.). (2020). *Bringing children back into the family, (Sociological Studies of Children and Youth v. 27)*. Emerald Publishing Limited.

Frankel, S., & Mountford, M. (2021). In search of meaningful participation: Making connections between emotions and learning. *Emotions, Space and Society*, 39. https://doi.org/10.1016/j.emospa.2021.100787

Frankl, V. E., Viktor, E., et al. (2004). *Man's search for meaning*. Rider.

Freire. (2021). https://www.freire.org/home. Accessed on March 29, 2023.

Frierson, P. R. (2022). *The Moral Philosophy of Maria Montessori: Agency and Ethical Life* (1st ed.). Bloomsbury Academic.

Gallwey, W. T. (1976). *Inner tennis: Playing the game* (1st ed.). Random House.

Gallwey, W. T. (1981). *The inner game of golf*. Random House.

Gatto, J. T. (2005). *Dumbing us down: The hidden curriculum of compulsory schooling*. New Society Publishers.

Giddens, A. (1979). *Central problems in social theory*. Macmillan.

Gilbert, I. (2013). *Essential motivation in the classroom*. Routledge/Falmer.

Gladwell, M. (2008). Acclaim for Malcolm Gladwell's Outliers. In *Outliers*. Little Brown & Company.

Global Partnership to End Violence Against Children. (2021). https://endcorporalpunishment.org/resources/global-report-2021/

Goodhart, D. (2020). *Head, Hand, Heart*. Allen Lane.

gov.uk. (24/11/2022). Permanent exclusions and suspensions in England. https://explore-education-statistics.service.gov.uk/find-statistics/permanent-and-fixed-period-exclusions-in-england

Galton, M., Gray, J., & McLaughlin, C. (2011). *The supportive school*. Cambridge Scholars Publishing.

Guardian. (2022a July, 13). https://www.theguardian.com/education/2022/jul/13/uk-schools-advised-to-assess-risk-of-strip-search-before-calling-police

Guardian. (2023, February 18). 'Unconscious bias training is 'nonsense', says outgoing race relations chair. https://www.theguardian.com/education/2023/feb/21/black-people-labelled-backward-as-children-seek-justice-for-lifelong-trauma. Accessed on February 27, 2023.

Guardian. (2021, October 19). Case closed': 99.9% of scientists agree climate emergency caused by humans. https://www.theguardian.com/environment/2021/oct/19/case-closed-999-of-scientists-agree-climate-emergency-caused-by-humans

Guardian. (2019, September 24). 'She seems very happy': Trump appears to mock Greta Thunberg's emotional speech https://www.theguardian.com/us-news/2019/sep/24/she-seems-very-happy-trump-appears-to-mock-greta-thunbergs-emotional-speech. Accessed on February 29, 2023.

Guardian. (2022, March 28). https://www.theguardian.com/us-news/2022/mar/28/dont-say-gay-bill-florida-ron-desantis

Haidt, J. (2021, July 31). This is our chance to pull teenagers out of the smartphone trap. *New York Times*.

Hart, R. (1992). *Children's participation: From tokenism to citizenship*. UNICEF International Child Development Centre.

Hattie, J. (2009). *Visible learning: A synthesis of meta-analysis relating to achievement*. Routledge.

Hattie, J. (2012). *Visible learning for teachers: Maximizing impact on learning*.

Hattie, & Larsen, S. N. (2020). *The purposes of education: A conversation between John Hattie and Steen Nepper Larsen*. Routledge.

Hay Group. (2002). *Maverick: Breakthrough leadership that transforms schools* (1st ed.). Hay Group Management Ltd.

Hendrick, H. (1997). Construction and reconstruction of British childhood: An interpretive survey, 1800 to the present. In A. James & A. Prout (Eds.), *Constructing and Reconstructing Childhood*. Falmer Press.

Hopkins, B. (2004). *Just Schools: A whole school approach to restorative justice*. Jessica Kingsley Publishers.

Hume, J. (2023). Hearing Children's Voices in the Forest. In S. Frankel (Ed.), *Establishing Child Centred Practice Part B*. Emerald Publishing Limited.

James, A. (1993). *Childhood Identities*. Edinburgh University Press.

James, A. L. (2010). Competition or integration? The next step in childhood studies? *Childhood, 17*(4), 485–499.

James, A. (2013). *Socialising children*. Palgrave Macmillan.

James, A., & James, A. L. (2004). *Constructing childhood*. Palgrave Macmillan.

James, A., Jenks, C., & Prout, A. (1998). *Theorising childhood*. Polity.

James, A., & Prout, A. (Ed.). (1997). *Constructing and reconstructing childhood*. Falmer Press. [first published 1990].

Jenks, C. (1996). *Childhood*. Routledge.

Kellaway, L. (2021). What is the point of schools. https://www.ft.com/content/13231302-8443-4652-b751-4082a936b282

Kets de Vries, M. (2019). *Down the Rabbit Hole*. Palgrave Macmillan.

Kholberg, L. (1984). *The psychology of moral development*. Harper & Row.

Kiel, F. (2015). *Return on character: The real reason leaders and their companies win*. Harvard Business Review Press.

King, R., & Peguero, A. A. (2018). The school to prison pipeline. In J. Deaken, E. Taylor, & A. Kupchik (Eds.), *The Palgrave International Handbook of School Discipline, Surveillance, and Social Control*. Palgrave Macmillan.

Kirtzinger, J. (2010). Who are you kidding? Children, power, and the struggle against sexual abuse. In K. Sternheimer (Ed.), *Childhood in American Society*. Allyn & Bacon.

Kline, N. (2020). *The promise that changes everything: I won't interrupt you*. Penguin.

Klocker, N. (2007). An example of "thin" agency: Child domestic workers in Tanzania. In R. Panelli, S. Punch, & E. Robson (Eds.), *Global perspectives on rural childhood and youth: Young rural lives*. Routledge.

Kohn, A. (2011). *Feel bad education*. Beacon Books.

Lachman, G. (2007). *Rudolf Steiner: An introduction to his life and work*. Jeremy P. Tarcher/Penguin.

Lakoff, G., & Johnson, M. (1980). *Metaphors we live by*. University of Chicago Press.

Lever, C. (2018). *Navigating change: A leaders guide*. Telios.

Levine, P. (2014, September 8). Jonathan Haidt's six foundations of morality. https://peterlevine.ws/?p=14220. Accessed on March 29, 2023.

Light, P. (1986). Context, conservation and conversation. In M. Richards & P. Light (Eds.), *(Des) Children of Social Worlds*. Polity Press.

Locke, J. (1998). *An essay concerning human understanding*. Wordsworth Classics.

Lucas, B., & Spencer, E. (2020). *Zest for learning: Developing curious learners who relish real world challenges*. Crown House Publishing.

Lukes, S. (2005). *Power: A radical view*. Palgrave Macmillan.

Lundy, L. (2018). In defence of tokenism? Implementing children's right to participate in collective decision-making. *Childhood*, 25(3), 340–354. https://doi.org/10.1177/0907568218777292

Macbeath, J. (1999). *Schools must speak for themselves*. Routledge.

de Mause, L. (1974). *The history of childhood*. Psychohistory Press.

Mayall, B. (1994). Children in action at home and school. In B. Mayall (Ed.), *Children's Childhoods*.

Mayall, B. (2002). *Towards a sociology for childhood*. Open University Press.

McCracken, J. (2016). *Clean language in the classroom*. Crown House Publishing.

Meintjes, H. (2014). Growing up in time of AIDS: The shinning recorders of Zisize. In K. Tisdall, A. Gadda, & U. Butler (Eds.), *Children and young people's participation and its transformative potential*. Palgrave Macmillan.

McNamee, S. (2016). *The social study of childhood*. Palgrave Macmillan.

Mountford, M. (2020). Beyond Yes and No: Practising consent in children's everyday lives. In S. Frankel & S. McNamee (Eds.), *Bringing children back into the family, sociological studies of childhood and youth* (Vol. 27). Emerald Publishing Limited.

MSBNC. (2023). School district name social media companies in mental health lawsuits. www.youtube.com/watch?v=0F7qYZOQWiw&list=TLPQMjAwMzIwMjPea3Qfm_lMlw&index=12. Accessed on March 29, 2023.

Muijs, D., & Bokhove, C. (2020). *Metacognition and self-regulation: Evidence review*. Education Endowment Fund.

Mulholland, K. (2023). Using pupil views templates to explore children's experiences of teaching and learning. In S. Frankel (Ed.), *Establishing Child Centred Practice Part B*. Emerald Publishing Limited.

NEU Survey. (2021). The state of education: Staff workload, wellbeing and retention. NEU. https://neu.org.uk/state-education-staff-workload-wellbeing-and-retention

New Economics Foundation. (2008). Five Ways to Wellbeing. https://neweconomics.org/2008/10/five-ways-to-wellbeing

Nye, J. (2008). *The power to lead Oxford*. Oxford University Press.

OECD. (2016). *Skills matter: Further results from the survey of adult skills, OECD skills studies*. OECD Publishing. https://doi.org/10.1787/9789264258051-en

OECD. (2020a). *Achieving the New Curriculum for Wales, Implementing Education Policies*. OECD Publishing. https://doi.org/10.1787/4b483953-en

OECD. (2020b). *OECD Skills Strategy Northern Ireland (United Kingdom): Assessment and Recommendations, OECD Skills Studies*. OECD Publishing. https://doi.org/10.1787/1857c8af-en

OECD 2023 'Starting Strong V1. https://www.oecd-ilibrary.org/sites/f47a06ae-en/index.html?itemId=/content/publication/f47a06ae-en

Orwell, G. (1949/[1984]). Secker and Warburg.

Parsons, T. (1951). *The social system*. Routledge and Megan Paul.

Patterson, T. (2018). *Social change theories in motion*. Routledge.

Pearson, G. (1983). *Hooligans: A history of respectable fears*. Macmillan.

Perkins, D. (1993). *Thinkgin connections: Earning to think and thinking to learn*. Addison-Wesley.

Perry, G. (2018). *The lost boys*. Scribe.

Piaget, J. (1935/[1975]). *The Moral Judgement of the Child*. Routledge and Kegan Paul.

Piaget, J. (1967). *Six psychological studies*. University of London Press.

Pollard, A. (1994). Towards a sociology of learning. In A. Pollard & J. Bounre (Eds.), *Teaching and Learning in the Primary School*. Rutledge.

Pollard, A. (2014). *Reflective teaching in schools.* Bloomsbury.

Rapport, N. (1995). Migrant selves and stereotypes. In S. Pile & N. Thrift (Eds.), *Mapping the subject.* Routledge.

Rauch, J. (2018). *The happiness curve: Why life gets better after midlife.* Bloomsbury.

Restrepo, S. (2019). *Brené Brown: The call to courage.* Netflix.

Rinaldi, C. (2006). *In dialogue with Reggio Emilia: Listening, researching and learning* (1st ed.). Routledge.

Ritchhart, R. (2015). *Creating cultures of thinking: The 8 forces we must master to truly transform our schools* (1st ed.). Jossey-Bass & Pfeiffer Imprints, Wiley.

Rittel, H. W. J., & Webber, M. M. (1973). Dilemmas in a general theory of planning. *Policy Sciences, 4*(2), 155–169.

Robinson, K. (2006). *Do schools kill creativity.* https://www.ted.com/talks/sir_ken_robinson_do_schools_kill_creativity

Robinson, & Aronica, L. (2013). *Finding your element: How to discover your talents and passions and transform your life.* Viking.

Robinson, & Aronica, L. (2016). *Creative schools.* Penguin Books.

Rogoff, B. (1990). *Apprenticeship in thinking: Cognitive development in social context.* Oxford University Press.

Russell, S. (2021). Living with artificial intelligence. BBC Reith Lectures. https://www.bbc.co.uk/programmes/articles/3pVB9hLv8TdGjSdJv4CmYjC/nine-things-you-should-know-about-ai

Russell, S. (2021a). Living with Artificial Intelligence: AI and the Economy. BBC Reith Lectures. https://www.bbc.co.uk/programmes/m0012fnc

Sachs, J. (2017). How we can face the future without fear. together – TED talk. https://www.ted.com/talks/rabbi_lord_jonathan_sacks_how_we_can_face_the_future_without_fear_together

Sachs, J. (2020). *Morality.* Hachette.

Saint-Exupéry, A. d. (1943). *The Little Prince.* Harcourt, Brace & World.

Sarason, S. B. (1996/[1971]). *Revisiting: The culture of the school and the problem of change.* Teachers College Press.

Scott, A., & Gratton, L. (2020). *The new long life: A framework for flourishing in a changing world*. Bloomsbury.

Shakespeare, W. (2005). *The complete works*. Oxford University Press.

Shier, H. (2001). Pathways to participation: Openings, opportunities and obligations. *Children & Society*, 15, 107–117.

Short, G. (1999). Children's grasp of controversial issues. In M. Woodhead (Ed.), *Making sense of social development*. Routledge.

Schutz, A., & Sandy, M. (2011). *Collective action for social change*. Palgrave Macmillan.

Skills Development Scotland. (2018). Skills 4.0: A skills model to drive Scotland's future – Skills Development Scotland. https://www.skillsdevelopmentscotland.co.uk/media/44684/skills-40_a-skills-model.pdf

Smith, M. (2017). *The Emotional learner*. Routledge.

Smout, T. (1969). *History of the Scottish People: 1560–1830*. Fontana Press.

Snyder, T. (2019). *The road to unfreedom*. Tim Duggan Books.

Sternberg, R. J. (2014). The development of adaptive competence. *Developmental Review*, 34, 208–224.

Sullivan, W., & Rees, J. (2008). *Clean language: Revealing metaphors and opening minds*. Crown Publishing.

Taft, J. K. (2019). *The kids are in charge activism and power in Peru's movement of working children*. New York University Press. https://doi.org/10.18574/9781479870554

TED. (2006). Do schools kill creativity. https://www.ted.com/talks/sir_ken_robinson_do_schools_kill_creativity

TED. (2010). The power of vulnerability. https://www.ted.com/talks/brene_brown_the_power_of_vulnerability/comments

The Children's Society. (2022). Good Childhood Report. https://www.childrenssociety.org.uk/information/professionals/resources/good-childhood-report-2022

The Conversation. (2017, January 10). What happened to our promised leisure time? (https://theconversation.com/what-happened-to-our-promised-leisure-time-and-will-we-find-it-in-the-smart-city-83570). Accessed on March 29, 2023.

Tibbits, F., & Bajaj, M. (2017). 'Evolution of Human Rights Education Models, Human Rights Education (pp. 69–95). University of Pennsylvania Press.

Tisdall, K., Gadda, A. M., & Butler, U. M. (2014). Introduction: People and young people's participation in collective decision making. In A. M. G. Tisdall & U. M. Butler (Eds.), *Children and young people's participation and its transformative potential: Learning from across countries*. Palgrave Macmillan.

Tsai, H.-H. (2013). Knowledge management vs. data mining: Research trend, forecast and citation approach. *Expert Systems with Applications, 40*(8), 3160–3173.

Turner, E. (2018). Commentary on Chapter 8: Children and death in the Canadian context. In S. Frankel & S. McNamee (Eds.), *Contextualising childhoods: Growing up in Europe and North America*. Palgrave Macmillan.

Twenge, J. M. (2006). *Generation me: Why today's young Americans are more confident, assertive, entitled-and more miserable-than ever before*. Free Press.

Twenge, J. M., Haidt, J., Blake, A. B., McAllister, C., Lemon, H., & Le Roy, A. (2021). Worldwide increases in adolescent loneliness. *Journal of Adolescence, 93*(Complete), 257–269. https://doi.org/10.1016/j.adolescence.2021.06.006

UN. (2019). The future is now: Science for achieving sustainable development.

UN. (2023). Sustainable development goals. https://sdgs.un.org/goals. Accessed on March 15, 2023.

UNICEF. (2020). Unicef report card 16. https://www.unicef.ca/en/unicef-report-card-16

Waldinger, R., & Schulz, M. (2023). *The good life: And how to live it*. Random House.

Walker, C. (2014). *From contempt to curiosity: Creating the conditions for groups to collaborate using clean language and systemic modelling*. Clean Publishing.

Walkerdine, V. (2009). Developmental psychology and the study of childhood. In M. J. Kehily (Ed.), *An introduction to childhood studies* (2nd ed.). Open University Press.

Wall, J. (2016). *Children's rights: Today's global challenge*. Rowman & Littlefield.

Watkins, C. (2005, March). Classrooms as learning communities: A review of research. *London Review of Education, 3*(1), 47–64.

Watkins, C. (2006). Personalised classroom learning. No. 29 INSI Research Matters International Network for School Improvement.

Watkins, C. (2008, March). Depoliticisation, demoralisation and depersonalisation – And how to better them. *Pastoral Care in Education, 26*(1), 5–11.

Watkins, C., Carnell, E., & Lodge, C. (2007). *Effective learning in classrooms*. Sage.

Watkins, C., Carnell, E., Lodge, C., Wagner, P., & Whalley, C. (2000). *Learning about learning: Resources for supporting effective learning*. Routledge.

Watkins, C., Wagner, P., & Whalley, C. (2000). *Learning about learning: Resources for supporting effective learning*. Routledge.

Welch, K., & Payne, A. A. (2018). Zero Tolerance school policies. In J. Deakin, E. Taylor, & A. Kupchik (Eds.), *The Palgrave International Handbook of School Discipline, Surveillance, and Social Control*. Palgrave Macmillan.

Weller, S. (2009). Exploring the Spatiality of participation: Teenagers' experiences in an English Secondary School. *Youth and Policy, 101*, 15–32.

White, S. (1996). Depoliticising development: The uses and abuses of participation. *Development in Practice, 6*(1), 6–15.

Wollstonecraft, M. (1792). *A vindication of the rights of woman*. Penguin.

Woodhead, M. (2009). Childhood studies past, present and future. In M. J. Kehily (Ed.), *An Introduction to childhood studies* (2nd ed.). OU Press.

World Economic Forum. (2023). https://www.weforum.org/focus/fourth-industrial-revolution. Accessed on March 15, 2023.

World Health Organization (WHO). Regional Office for Europe. (2020). *Spotlight on adolescent health and well-being. Findings from the 2017/2018 Health Behaviour in School-aged Children (HBSC) survey in Europe and Canada. International report. Volume 1. Key findings*. World Health Organization. Regional Office for Europe. https://apps.who.int/iris/handle/10665/332091

Zimmerman, B. J. (2002). Becoming a self-regulated learner: An overview. *Theory Into Practice, 41*(2), 64–70.

INDEX

Adaptability, 138
Adaptive competence, 58–59
Age, 36
Agency, 48
AI, 61
Allowing learning, 134–135
Anthropology, 44–45
Assumption tracker, 98–101
Authoritarianism, growth of, 3–4

Biological maturation, 36–37
Body, 81–82

Capacity, 144
Capital, 82–83
Change, 23
'Charismatic leader' centre, 138
Child/childhood/children
    competence, 46
    experiences, 46, 57
    history of, 55
    rights, 21–22
    studies, 55
Children's grasp of controversial issues, 37
Citizenship education, 126–127
Classroom engagement, 133
Clean language, 116–118
Climate of acceptance, 74–76
Co-participation, 121
Co-production, 122
Coaching, 135
Cognitive ability, 56–58, 61
Cognitive Ability Tests (CATests), 56–57
Compliance, 161
Compulsory schooling, 39, 54

Connected learners, 12, 127, 141–142, 144–145
    case for, 6–7
Connected learning approach, 23–24
Connectedness, 13–16
Continuing professional development (CPD), 111
Conversations, 103
Corporal punishment, 39–41
COVID-19 pandemic, 28
Creative Schools, 17–18
Culture for learning, 103
    community task, 107
    idea, 104
    motivations, 106
    rhetoric *vs.* reality, 109
    talk, listen and plan, 104–107
Culture of advocacy, 20
Curriculum design, 37

Demoralisation, 59
Depersonalisation, 59
Depoliticisation, 59
Developing questions, 117
Discipline, re-imagining, 84–86
Disconnected learner, 16–17, 104–105
Dominant assumption, 34, 38, 42

Education, 60
Educationalists, 133
Educator, 1
Effective learning, 50
    connections, 103
Emotional bank account, 15
Emotional intelligence, 161

Emotions, 119–121
Empathetic executives, 138
Empathy, 138
Ethos, 114
Explicit conversations, 145

Fabric of childhood, 48
Facilitators, 1, 133–135
Flow, 62–63

Gender, 35–36
Global warming, 6
Guided participation, 145

Habitus, 82
Human skills, 61–62

Individual, 43, 45, 141
 learning capabilities, 142–143
Inspire lead learners (*see also* Learners), 133
 idea, 133
 impact, 139–140
 research, 139
 talk, listen and plan, 134–139
Inspiring Schools, 21
Instructor, 1
Intelligence Quotient (IQ), 56–58
Intention questions, 117
Interpersonal skills, 161

Language for learning, 114–116
Learners, 1, 33, 69, 141–142
 with agency, 44–45
 as becoming, 34–37
 case for connected learners, 6–7
 identities, 159–160
 as malleable, 42–44
 meaning maker, 47–49
 new paradigm, 44–45
 as ominous, 38–41
 perspectives, 34
 re-imagining child, 45–46
Learning, 1, 9, 33–34, 53, 69
 with agency, 49–51
 attributes, 114
 capabilities, 142–143

challenges, 1
changing world, 10
climate of acceptance, 74–76
connectedness, 13–16
connection continuum, 28–30
 by control, 70–76
framework, 67–68
global influences and impacts, 11
identifying disconnection from learning, 27–28
identity, 1
journeys, 159–160
 to learn, 63–68
lifelong journey, 12–13
as navigation, 59, 62, 161
opportunity, 76–77
passion for, 1–2
as performance, 56–59
positive learning identity, 12
potential, 143–146
rules, 70–72
seven ages, 13
spaces, 110
standardised society, 54–55
surveillance, 72–74
time for change, 2–6
value, voice and vision, 16
work, 62–63
Learning by consent, 70, 76, 86
 being known and understood, 76–77
 feelings, 77–78
 filtering feelings, 79–84

Meaning maker, 47–49
Meaningful opportunities, 125, 127–128, 130
 change, 130
 creating, 128
 design and deliver, 129
 idea, 125
 talk, listen and plan, 125–130
 thinking, 125–127
Mental Health, 4–5
Meta-learning, 142

Metaphors, 113–114
Modus operandi (MO), 3
Moments of 'readiness', 37
Motivations, 106

Narrative, 160–162
National Citizen Service (NCS), 125–126
Navigators of learning, 64
Non-verbal language, 122–123

Obedience, 70, 76, 161
'Organised' learning, 105–106
Outdoor learning, 133

Participation, 121
Passion for learning, 1–2
Piaget's model, 36–37
Positive feedback loops, 130
Positive learning identity, 12
Post-truth, 3
Potentiality, 144
Power, 79–81
   assumptions, 93–94, 96
   idea, 93
   talk, listen and plan, 93–97
   thinking, 96–97
   of words, 113–114
Predictability, 54
'Prevent' initiative, 72–73
Programme for International Student Assessment (PISA), 4–5
Provide, protect, profit, participation (4P), 106

Race, 35–36
Rational thought, 35
Reason, 35–36
Research and inquiry, 121–122
Resulting practice, 34, 38, 42
Ripple effect, 139
Risk management, 138
Rule-based learning, 71

Scholastic Aptitude Tests (SATests), 56–57

School, 17–18, 39, 55
   councils, 21
   loneliness, 4–5
Schooling, 55
'Schools with spirit', 138
Self regulated learning (SRL), 135–136
Self-confidence, 127
Self-esteem, 127
Self-respect, 127
Sequence questions, 117
Shinning Recorders of Zisize in South Africa, The, 20–21
Social capital, 82–84
Social interaction, 61
Social Media, 4–5
Social structure, 42–43
Social world, 94–95
Socialisation, 43–44
Sociology, 42–43
Standardised society, 54–55
Stereotypes, 94–95
Stimulus-response, 44–45
Surveillance, 72–74

Tame problems, 5
Teacher, 1
   pupil engagement, 126–127
Technical vocabulary, 118–123
Transactional leadership, 138
Transformational leadership, 138

UK system, 56
UN Sustainable Development Goals, 11
Unchangeable intelligence, 58
Uniformity, 54
Unifying language, 113
   idea, 113
   talk, listen and plan, 113–123

Values, 9, 16, 19, 114, 134, 136
   creating capabilities to narrate and navigate learning journey, 18–19

sense of agency and purpose, 16–18
Virtue education, 38–39, 41
Vision, 9, 16, 23, 26, 138–139
  awareness of capacity to take control of learning journey, 23–25
  creating capabilities to identify pathways, 25–26
Vocabulary, 123

Voice, 9, 16, 19, 22, 136–137
  creating capabilities, 21–22
  realisation contribution counts and feelings matter, 19–21

White populations, 35–36
Wicked problems, 5–6

Zero tolerance, 73–74

Printed and bound by CPI Group (UK) Ltd, Croydon, CR0 4YY
31/10/2023

08158609-0001